CHESTER
AD 400-1066
FROM ROMAN FORTRESS
TO ENGLISH TOWN

CHESTER
AD 400-1066
FROM ROMAN FORTRESS
TO ENGLISH TOWN

DAVID MASON

TEMPUS

First published 2007

Tempus Publishing Limited
The Mill, Brimscombe Port,
Stroud, Gloucestershire, GL5 2QG
www.tempus-publishing.com

British Library Cataloguing in Publication Data.
A catalogue record for this book is available from the British Library.

ISBN 978-0-7524-4100-9

Typesetting and origination by Tempus Publishing Limited
Printed in Great Britain

CONTENTS

PREFACE

If I had attempted to write this book at the start of my archaeological career more than 30 years ago it would have been a very slim volume indeed. Not simply because of the inadequacies of my own knowledge but primarily because there was little archaeological evidence available other than a few coin-hoards, a small quantity of pottery and one set of features to flesh out the bare bones of the references to Chester in the historical sources. The production of a far more substantial work has been made possible by the vast quantity of new information that has come to light since then; so vast in fact that it has completely transformed our knowledge of early medieval Chester, or at least the period after the founding of the *burh* in 907. This new information derives variously from archaeological excavation, from historical research and from chance finds of artefacts, but principally from the first of these.

What one might call the breakthrough discovery came with the Lower Bridge Street excavations of 1974-6 when the first buildings of Anglo-Saxon date to be identified in Chester were found. Further discoveries relating to the tenth and eleventh centuries – and occasionally earlier periods – followed soon afterwards as a number of sites were excavated within the area of the former legionary fortress, giving a useful spatial distribution of information across the city and complimenting the well-known historical evidence indicating Chester's position as the pre-eminent administrative and commercial centre in north-western England in the late Anglo-Saxon period. Sometimes the date of buildings and structures was recognised at the time of excavation and sometimes this only became apparent as the analysis of data was carried out once an excavation had finished. In addition, further information was forthcoming as the records of unpublished sites excavated years earlier were worked over for the purpose of preparing a series of synoptic reports dealing with pre- and post-1973 sites under an English Heritage sponsored Backlog Project.

It is doubtful whether the enormous advances in our knowledge and understanding of the period covered by this book would have been possible had not the City Council taken the enlightened decision to maintain its own Archaeology Service since the early 1970s. Such continuity has enabled its staff to build up a body of knowledge, expertise and insight that would not have been possible otherwise; something that is absolutely essential not only for advancing understanding of complex multi-period urban archaeology but also for determining how best to protect and manage this precious resource in situations where it is subject to intense development pressures.

There is still much to learn, however, even for the period 900–1066, which is the one for which we have the most evidence. This is even truer for the three centuries before this, when Chester lay in English Mercia, and the two centuries before that again of the sub-Roman and Dark Age times. Despite the enormous amount of investigation undertaken since the early 1970s, whether research-inspired or development-led, we still have only a handful of artefacts and archaeological features attributable to this 500 year period in Chester's history. As far as artefacts are concerned the situation is unlikely to improve given that mass-produced goods, at least non-perishable types, simply didn't exist in western Britain. Occasionally, carefully targeted research can produce extremely important results and in this regard the author's work with the Chester Archaeological Society at Heronbridge in recent years has proved particularly fruitful for the light it has shed on known historical events at Chester in the opening years of the seventh century.

Having been involved in the investigation of Chester's archaeology for more years than I now care to remember, and having been privileged to have participated directly in some of the major discoveries relating to the period under discussion, it has been a pleasure to have the opportunity to draw together all the disparate strands of evidence into something which hopefully resembles a coherent narrative. That this cannot in any way be described as a definitive work highlights the most exciting aspect of its subject: there is still so much to discover.

ACKNOWLEDGEMENTS

I should like to express my thanks to Chester City Council for permission to reproduce many of the images featured within this book. I am particularly grateful to the following officers of the Council for their assistance in this regard: Steve Woolfall (Museum Services Officer) along with Mike Morris (City Archaeologist), Peter Carrington (Senior Archaeologist – Post-Excavation) and Cheryl Quinn (Illustration Officer) of Chester Archaeology.

An overview of this kind inevitably draws heavily upon the work of others and in this case most especially that of Simon Ward (Senior Archaeologist, Chester Archaeology). Thanks are also due to Dan Garner (Chester Archaeology) and Tony Wilmott (English Heritage) for taking the time to discuss with me on site the results of the recent excavations at the amphitheatre site.

I am also indebted to The British Museum, The Chester Archaeological Society, Cheshire County Council and York Osteoarchaeology Ltd for permission to reproduce images which are in their ownership.

This book includes much new information about the least understood period in Chester's long history and none more topical than the dramatic discoveries made at Heronbridge, just south of the city, as a consequence of the author's research project with the Chester Archaeological Society in recent years. That work would not have been possible without the unstinting efforts of the many volunteers who took part in the project both actively in the field and in a supporting role. Those worthy of special mention are Averil Downs, Carolyne Kershaw, Celia Kinnersley, Debbie Morton, Georgina Muskett, Marlene Nolan, Catherine Roberts, Gina Siddons, Richard Brenton, Eric Evans, George Storey, the late John Tindall and Edwin Warwick. My deepest thanks also go to Pat Frost who foolishly allowed herself to be talked into supervising this motley crew of field workers.

I am grateful to those members of staff at Tempus Publishing directly involved in bringing this project to fruition, particularly Tom Vivian and Tom Sunley. Finally, I should like to thank Peter Kemmis Betty for commissioning this book and thus giving me the opportunity to describe another period of Chester's long and fascinating history.

THE END OF EMPIRE: LATE ROMAN CHESTER

In *City of the Eagles*, the author's first book for Tempus on the archaeology and history of Chester, the story was told of the city's development from its foundation as a Roman legionary base under the Emperor Vespasian, through its evolution into a garrison city in the third century and on to its eventual decline during the decades either side of AD 400. There was much evidence and many themes to accommodate within the space allowed by the publisher and it was inevitable that some periods of *Deva*'s long history would receive more attention than others. In effect, and particularly because of the author's concern to convey his views on the possible special role planned for Chester at the time of its foundation, this meant that there was a heavy emphasis on the earlier part of *Deva*'s history. This may have detracted from the book's usefulness for some readers but it did leave open the possibility of taking another look at the evidence for late Roman Chester by way of a scene-setting, introductory chapter in any sequel, and that is precisely what the reader will find in the first chapter of this book. Obviously, to try to understand what may have happened in Chester in the fifth century – and because of the dearth of evidence it has to be 'may' rather than 'did' – it is necessary to know how events affected *Deva* during the century leading up to Britain's severance from the Roman Empire.

Although, unlike the following two centuries, we do at least have substantive archaeological evidence for occupation in the fourth century, it must be admitted that a precise definition of Chester's role and character in this period is beyond our present understanding. Was it still a legionary fortress after 300? Was it still a military base but with a different garrison? Was the military presence drastically reduced so that it became more like a town with a garrison attached? Was there still a military unit here at the end of the fourth century? All of these are pertinent questions given the many changes that affected both the army and urban society in the fourth century as the Empire struggled to cope with both external pressures and internal strains. They are also questions which to a great extent remain unanswered.

The latest evidence for the Twentieth Legion's presence at Chester consists of tiles bearing the legionary stamp with the suffix *DE*, interpreted by some as an abbreviation of the honorific title *Deciana* bestowed by the Emperor Trajan Decius (249-51). It is equally possible, however, that this abbreviation stands for *Devana*, the legion having added the place-name *Deva* to its titles. If so, this would make the tiles undatable, although as this was generally a late practice the tiles could still belong to the third or even the fourth century. A vexillation of *Legio XX* is attested at Mainz in 255[1] and a few years later a joint vexillation of *Legio XX* and *Legio II Augusta* was in Pannonia.[2] The latest reference to the legion anywhere occurs on coins struck between 287 and 293 by Carausius, who set up a separate 'empire' in Britain and Gaul. Carausius was murdered and succeeded by Allectus, his finance minister, who ruled for a further three years before Britain was retaken for Rome by Constantius Chlorus, father of Constantine the Great. The later history of the Twentieth is unknown: it may have continued in existence without leaving any further memorials; it may have been disbanded; it may have been broken up into smaller units with different titles; or it may have been destroyed. The legion does not appear in the late fourth-century inventory of military units known as the *Notitia Dignitatum*, but as the section dealing with Britain fails to mention any garrisons in either Wales or in north-west England south of Lancaster it is possible that the relevant part of the document was lost or misplaced during the original compilation.

The archaeological evidence compensates to some extent for the lack of references in the documentary sources and an absence of epigraphic material. Excavations carried out over the last 40 years have shown that there was a very considerable amount of rebuilding and refurbishment inside the fortress at some stage during the opening decades of the fourth century (see *1* for location of the legionary fortress in relation to the modern city and *2* for the position and identity of individual fortress buildings). In the fortress baths, for example, most of the hypocaust systems throughout the entire complex were replaced and there was extensive remodelling of the accommodation and facilities in the *caldarium*.[3] The more modest bath-building beside the Elliptical Building underwent a similarly extensive reconstruction of its heating system and minor alterations were also made to the Elliptical Building itself.[4] Both the *principia* and the enormous store-building behind it were provided with new floorings in the early fourth century along with some modifications to their internal arrangements.[5] When it comes to the barracks, the accommodation for seven of the total of ten cohorts has been sampled so far and of these four were certainly

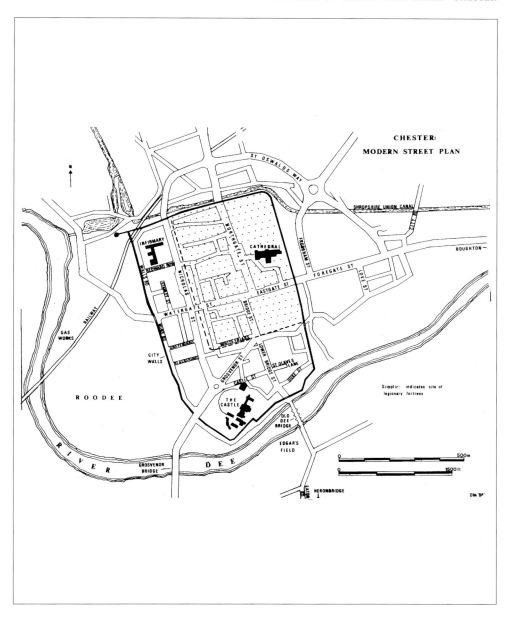

1 Modern Chester with area of Roman legionary fortress shaded

occupied down to at least the middle of the fourth century, albeit in some cases not continuously.[6] Only the granaries near the west gate appear not to have outlasted the end of the third century, but the evidence there is open to more than one interpretation.[7]

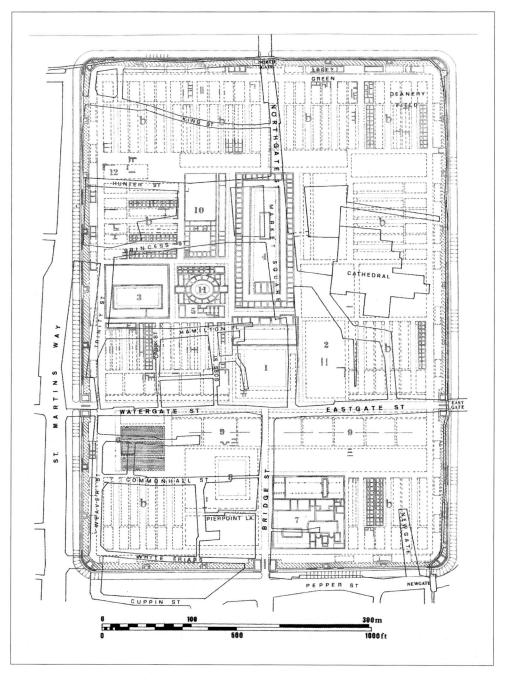

2 Plan showing position of fortress buildings and streets in relation to modern Chester
Key: b – barracks; 1 – headquarters building; 2 – commandant's residence; 3 – workshops; 4 – stores building; 5 – bath-building associated with the Elliptical Building; 6 – granaries; 7 – fortress baths; 8 – hospital; 9 – tribunes' houses; 10 – stores building; 11 – the Elliptical Building; 12 – granary

Thus there is plenty of evidence for there having been a major investment in the fortress and its facilities in the early fourth century on a scale and of a type which can only have been implemented by the military. Some of the works were so extensive as to suggest they were necessitated by something other than the normal replacement of infrastructure worn out through use and age. This is suggested in particular by evidence from the defences, which shows there was a rebuilding, usually from the base course of the curtain wall, around at least 50% of the perimeter following a period of neglect in which the fortress ditch was allowed to become filled with silt up to ground level and the fabric of the curtain wall itself began to deteriorate.[8] The suspension of routine maintenance had obviously lasted for many years and may have affected the wall itself, thus explaining the need for such an extensive reconstruction (the evidence is discussed in greater detail in chapter six in connection with the post-Roman history of Chester's defences). Perhaps, therefore, a considerable proportion of the legion was absent for much of the second half of the third century. Reference has already been made to one or more vexillations serving abroad and we know that there were detachments of the Twentieth serving at both Corbridge and Carlisle during the third century. Also, one imagines that Carausius and Allectus, faced with the threat of invasion from the Continent, would have transferred the bulk of the island's garrison from the north down to the south-east coast. Similar redeployments may have occurred earlier during the 14-year period 260-274 when Britain formed part of the breakaway 'Gallic Empire' initiated by Postumus.

A fascinating aspect of the rebuilding of the fortress wall is that it incorporated in its core fragments of tombstones and other funerary monuments taken from the cemeteries which surrounded the fortress and its civilian suburbs. It was the recovery of such material during repairs to the north wall in the late nineteenth century that endowed the city with its marvellous collection of Roman inscriptions and funerary sculpture.[9] However, the fact that those who rebuilt the fortress wall in the fourth century were prepared to desecrate the memorials of earlier legionaries and their families might indicate that it was not the Twentieth that was undertaking the work. There can be no certainty on this point though, given that many of the men serving with the Twentieth in the early fourth century may have had no familial connection with Chester. Whether or not the unit in residence was the Twentieth Legion, it was clearly a substantial force. This is indicated for example by the continuing maintenance of the fortress baths in their entirety, even allowing for the possibility that they were now also used by the civilian population. There was a tendency in the fourth century to split legions into a number of vexillations, which in time became legions in their own right, each having a strength of perhaps only 1,000 men, so there need be no surprise if not all of the Chester barracks were recommissioned in the fourth century. A further complication is the possibility that quarters were now provided for married men to live with their families inside the fortress, although it must be stressed that there is as yet no definite proof for this.

One other matter that ought to receive brief mention at this point is the possibility that part or all of the suburbs around the fortress were protected by defences in the later Roman period. Lengths of ditches with dimensions appropriate to a defensive purpose have been found close to the outer edge of the built-up area east of the fortress but in no case has a date or function been confirmed.[10] To the west of the fortress, running at the foot of the ancient river-cliff beside what is now the Roodee racecourse, is a wall of massive masonry. Traced over a distance of more than 250m this has traditionally been regarded as a quay wall (3). However, doubts have been expressed as to the validity of this interpretation and it may in fact have been a defensive wall erected, most probably, in the third century.[11] If so, and assuming it was not an additional military compound, then it is most likely to have linked up with the fortress defences at the north-east and north-west corners. There is the less likely possibility that this wall continued southwards to enclose in addition all of the area south of the fortress, in which case the line of the town wall, thought to have originated in the tenth or eleventh century, would actually have been established in the Roman period.

As one might expect from its strategic location, Chester's military significance clearly persisted long into the fourth century, even if its garrison was substantially reduced. Its role as a transhipment centre for goods on their way to the northern frontier would have continued and its related importance as a naval base would also have remained unchanged and possibly increased given the rising incidence of seaborne raiding along the west coast. Its workshops and armouries were also presumably kept busy supplying the garrisons in the north. While the possible absence of much of the garrison in the later third century may have had economic and social repercussions for the civilian population beside the fortress, there was renewed building activity around 300, including the erection of completely new buildings in the commercial quarter outside the east gate. Clearly the town, just like the fortress, was given a new lease of life.

Tending to the spiritual needs of both soldiers and civilians, as well as to the more down-to-earth requirements of their own organisation, would have been members of the growing body of Christian clergy. Constantine made Christianity the state religion in 312 and already by 314 all four provinces of Britain were able to send representatives to the Council of Arles. By the second half of the fourth century the number of bishops in Britain may have run into double figures.[12] Given its prominence and deeply Roman culture, Chester would have had the

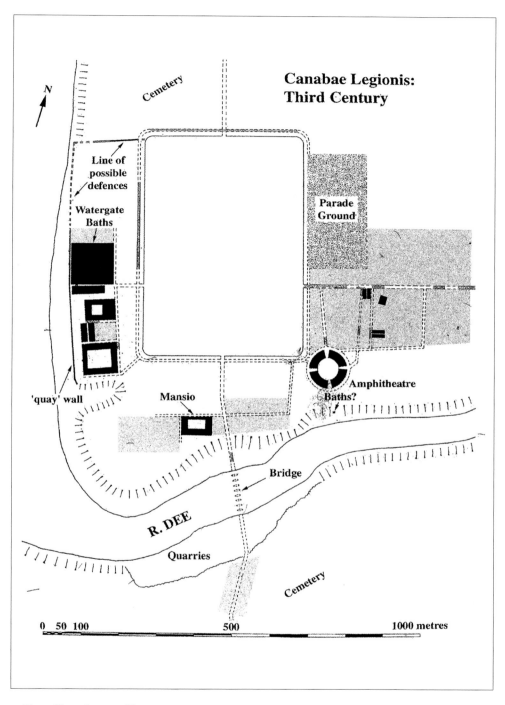

N

**Canabae Legionis:
Third Century**

Cemetery

Line of
possible
defences

Watergate
Baths

Parade
Ground

Amphitheatre
Baths?

'quay' wall

Mansio

Bridge

R. DEE

Quarries

Cemetery

0 50 100   500   1000 metres

3 Plan of later Roman Chester
Solid black – known buildings; shaded area – general extent of built-up area

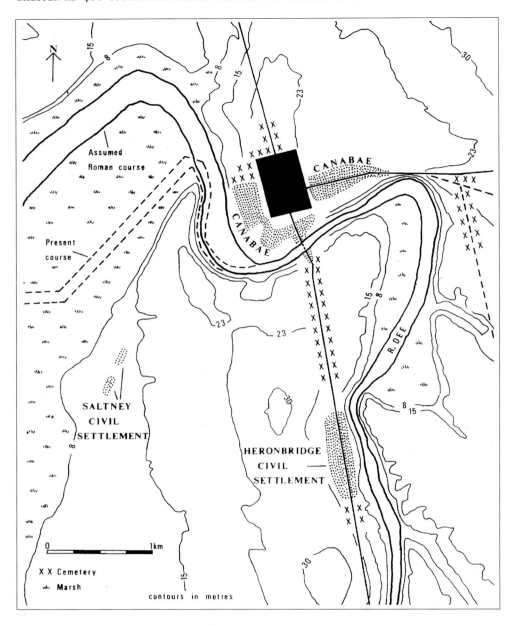

4 Roman Chester and its principal 'satellite' settlements

largest Christian community outside of Wroxeter and Carlisle, and possibly larger than either of these given that a higher proportion of its population had close ties to the state. The legionary shrine in the *principia* would have taken on a new religious aspect, being the repository of the standards, the symbols of the Roman state and of allegiance to the emperor, who henceforth – apart from one or two recidivists – was also the head of the Christian Church. But there may also have been at least one church building, possibly situated inside the fortress. The medieval chroniclers of St Werburgh's Abbey held that when the relics of St Werburgh were transferred here in 874 they were placed in an existing church on the site of high antiquity dedicated to SS Peter & Paul.[13] Whether or not there was any basis in fact for this assertion, the choice of Chester as the setting for an important synod *c.*601 suggests it had an ancient lineage as a high-status Christian site.[14]

The recent discovery of a number of salt-pans at Shavington, near Crewe, may have a bearing on this topic.[15] Two of them bear moulded inscriptions in low relief: on one is the name FL(AVIUS) VIVENTIUS and on the other the phrase VIVENTI [EPIS]COPI. Viventius was a common name among the Christian community and the word *episcopus* has been taken to mean 'bishop,' although it can also mean bailiff or steward. Devices on the pans may be crude versions of Christian symbols including the *crux decussata* (St Andrew's cross) and the *iota-chi*. There seems a strong possibility that salt manufacture from the local brine springs was under the control of the local bishop, presumably based at Chester. Just as in later times, the Church in the fourth century benefited from state endowments along with gifts from individuals. Furthermore, the discovery of a sixth- or seventh-century pennanular brooch only a few metres away from one of the pans points to this industry continuing in some form throughout the long period between the severance from Rome in 410 and the re-emergence of Chester into the historical record at the beginning of the seventh century.

Analysis of the coinage from Chester indicates a significant drop in the supply of coin around 350 compared with many other military sites and it may be there was a further reduction in the garrison at this time.[16] It has been suggested this may have been connected with the withdrawal of troops from Britain by Magnentius, the usurper emperor in the West, for his battle against Constantius II, emperor in the East.[17] In the battle fought at Mursa, in Pannonia, Magnentius was defeated, but both sides each lost more than 25,000 men and so the Empire was the main loser. Occupation of the fortress continued as is evidenced by pottery and smaller numbers of coins. Apart from a few coins, there is little sign of occupation in the civil settlement beside the fortress continuing much beyond 350. Both the *mansio* south of the fortress, which provided free lodgings for government officials as well as accommodation for paying guests, and shops along the road beyond the east gate were abandoned around this time.[18] At the amphitheatre some of the entrances were blocked up in the fourth century, giving rise to the suggestion that the building was turned into a defended citadel like some of its counterparts in other provinces.[19] Then again, the same phenomenon occurred at the Caerleon amphitheatre, but there it is known that the former passageways were converted into shrines or extra storage areas.[20] Similarly, a timber structure found at the centre of the arena during the 1960s excavation and now proposed as a possible Dark Age timber hall could just as easily have been some form of temporary structure erected in connection with celebrations on the occasion of King Edgar's visit to nearby St John's in 973.[21]

Possibly the widespread barbarian incursion of 367 resulted in the entire population of the suburbs moving inside the fortress. It may have been around this time that short sections of the north and west fortress walls underwent a further rebuilding. Alterations to internal buildings certainly continued to be made. The Elliptical Building baths, for example, underwent further modifications dated by coins to the period 364-75 or a little later, and the main fortress baths were also modified at some point in the second half of the fourth century.[22] A courtyard building on the opposite side of the *via praetoria* to the main baths was occupied down to the end of the fourth century. In its final years, however, the normal standards of cleanliness and hygiene were being abandoned, as evidenced by the fact that discarded bone left from the butchery of cattle was allowed to accumulate on its courtyard surfacing.[23] The usurper Magnus Maximus must have taken a considerable proportion of the forces still in Britain with him to the Continent in 383-4 for his ultimately unsuccessful bid for the throne, and withdrawals by other imperial adventurers occurred in the early years of the fifth century. The coin list at Chester suggests there were still troops (or perhaps just state officials) here receiving government pay in the 390s, but in what number is impossible to gauge.

To compensate for the withdrawal of regular troops from Wales it is possible that Maximus, or one of his immediate successors, replaced them with one or more tribes from areas just outside the province, giving them land in return for their defending it against raiders and other would-be settlers; a practice commonplace in this period all along the Empire's frontiers. There is a story in the Irish sources known as 'The Expulsion of the Desi' which records how a certain Eochaid took his people across the sea to settle in the territory of Demed (Dyfed), an event which probably occurred at some time in the decades around 400.[24] Other sources, both Irish and Welsh, also refer to Irish settlement as well as subsequent fighting between the two peoples and, as we shall see in the next chapter, there is plentiful archaeological and place-name evidence for Irish settlement in south-west Wales in the fifth and sixth centuries.[25] The fact that the name of Eochaid's great-grandson is recorded as Triphun – perhaps a corrupted version of the Roman army rank of tribune – while Triphun's son was called Aircol – perhaps derived from the Roman name Agricola – lends weight to this hypothesis. There is a parallel tradition for north-west Wales, where early sources (i.e. seventh century or earlier) used by the writer Nennius and folk memories preserved in medieval Welsh romance assert a connection between Maximus ('Macsen Wledig') and the early kingdoms in the region. In particular, they tell how Cunedda/Cunedag left that part of the Gododdin known as Manau in south-east Scotland and migrated to Wales accompanied by all of his sons except the eldest, who stayed behind to rule in his father's place.[26] It is recorded how Cunedda beat off Irish attacks and how, on his death, his realm was divided up between his sons, who went on to found independent kingdoms. Interestingly, Cunedda's father and grandfather had Roman names – Uetern (Aeternus) and Patern Pasrut (Paternus of the 'Red Cloak,' the latter perhaps a symbol of delegated imperial authority?).

By the opening years of the fifth century Chester's population may have been seriously reduced from what it had been only 25 years earlier. Troop withdrawals, either by the central authorities to reinforce the frontier in other provinces or by imperial adventurers, must have seriously depleted the strength of the army and almost certainly any naval forces available for Britain's defence. By this period, the families of serving soldiers were regarded as part and parcel of the 'regiment' and, at least on some occasions and in some parts of the Empire, the state provided or paid for their transportation (just like their food supplies) when it was redeployed.[27] Thus any official garrison reduction would have had an immediate and very significant impact on the population level, as well as on those people such as traders who depended indirectly upon soldiers' pay. Consequently, compared with the early third century, when *Deva's* total population probably numbered between ten and twelve thousand, it may have been only a fifth or even a tenth of that by 410 when the authorities in Britain made their unsuccessful appeal for help to the Emperor Honorius. However, while Chester's decline would have been a cause of much sadness and apprehension for many, especially those still resident, the reduction in the size of the population may actually have made it easier for the community to sustain itself through the uncertain times that lay ahead.

GENTLY SLUMBERING THROUGH THE DARK

The period between the end of Roman Britain and the emergence of Anglo-Saxon England (for ease of reference c.AD 410–c.AD 600) used to be referred to as the 'Dark Ages.' It is now usually described by the more general term of the 'early medieval period,' yet this change in terminology should not be interpreted as a sign that the gloom has lifted to any significant extent. Throughout large areas of Britain most of the normally commonplace means of identifying and dating human activity are absent. The mass production of everyday items, taken for granted only a few decades before, ceased soon after AD 400 and so pottery, metalwork and glassware are rare outside those parts of the country settled by the Anglo-Saxons. Small quantities of these goods were imported to western Britain from Gaul and the Mediterranean, but these only reached a few high-status sites.[1] Coinage gave way to barter and, apart from the occasional long-distance connection like that just mentioned, trade became far more localised and parochial. Official inscriptions of the imperial type were no longer commissioned, although memorials commemorating rulers or other prominent members of society were erected by Christian communities in Wales and the South West.[2] The dedications are in Latin and the phraseology employed on those in north-west Wales suggests continuing links with Gaul. Many of those in south Wales and south-west England carry bilingual dedications in Latin and the Irish Ogham script, or simply Ogham alone, and attest the presence of Irish settlers in this area, as does place-name evidence.[3]

Manuscript sources for this period do exist. There is the *De Excidio Britonum* (*On the Ruin of Britain*) written at some time in the first half of the sixth century by the British monk Gildas.[4] This was used extensively by Bede 200 years later in his *Ecclesiastical History of the English Speaking People*.[5] The next major work in chronological sequence is the anonymous *British Historical Miscellany*, often attributed to its suggested compiler Nennius in the ninth century.[6] Finally, there are the earliest sections of the annals contained in the *Anglo-Saxon Chronicle* which survives as seven complete and two fragmentary texts.[7] These were all written much later than the events they describe by people with particular and far from unbiased points of view, while the versions we possess have come down to us as copies of copies of copies and they undoubtedly contain errors and variations of interpretation introduced during the transcription process. Similarly, the Welsh source material consists predominantly of bardic poetry, the purpose of which was not the presentation of an accurate narrative but the celebration of the achievements of the aristocratic class in general and those of the individual poet's patron in particular. Such poetry harked back to pre-Roman Celtic tradition and, as Jackson put it, '… was recited orally to the assembled company in the chief's hall; and was handed down orally, being learnt by heart by subsequent reciters and so passed on for generations; and … all this was fostered and practised by the institutions of "bardic schools" in which budding poets were given an elaborate training in their profession, in oral composition of poetry and its recitation and transmission when learnt by heart'.[8] Despite the care with which such material was committed to memory, the opportunities for embellishment, confusion and distortion over time were obviously rife. As some dynasties died out or were supplanted and discredited material would have been altered with achievements and attributes perhaps assigned to others. Separating fact from fiction is thus very difficult, and often impossible. Choosing whether to accept or to reject events as they are described is usually down to the individual's professional evaluation of the balance of probability in the light of the available evidence. To express this in more cynical terms, it might be said that archaeologists and historians studying this period believe what they want to believe and reject the rest. Some scholars have expressed doubts as to whether certain major events in the sources actually happened, or were merely invented to make a political or religious point to the reader, and given the dubious reliability of the manuscripts this is a perfectly valid attitude. However, that said, there are instances where an event is described in a variety of independent sources, thus validating its occurrence. Also, as described in the next chapter, there are rare occasions when archaeology confirms in a very dramatic way that a specific event described in the sources really did take place.

As the governmental and socio-economic structures of Roman Britain disintegrated it would have been only natural for the more traditional forms of rule to reassert themselves; in other words, the fragmentation of the British provinces into smaller units and the emergence of chiefs and kings to fill the power vacuum. We know nothing of the details of the process, but we do have evidence that a pattern of kingdoms had become established in the West during the fifth century. They are listed by Gildas, who wrote his *De Excidio* in the first half of the sixth century, and their rulers are described by him as '*tyranni.*' From the manner in which Gildas describes them it seems that the most powerful of these kingdoms was Gwynedd, consisting of north-west Wales, then ruled by Maelgwn or Maglocunus the 'Dragon of the Island' (Anglesey). Bordering Gwynedd to the east was *Din Eirth*, probably named after Dinarth, near Deganwy, on the east bank of the lower Conwy where its ruler Cuneglasus had his court.[9] The eastern and southern boundaries of this kingdom (later to become known as Powys) are not known precisely but, at its greatest extent in the early to mid-seventh century, may well have included the western portion of both Shropshire and Cheshire (see below). However, in the period under discussion these areas may well have belonged to a separate kingdom. A document with late seventh-century origins known as the Tribal Hidage contains a list of peoples paying tribute to Mercia, along with the size of their lands measured in hides.[10] In its primary form, the list is headed by a people called the *Wrocensaetna* (literally 'people of the Wrocen') and their territory is by far the largest at 7,000 hides. Like the hill known as the Wrekin and the village known as Wroxeter, Wrocen is a name that derives from *Uriconium*, the tribal capital and administrative centre of the Cornovii in the Roman period, situated 8km east of modern Shrewsbury. The other early medieval kingdoms of *Lindesfaran* and the *Magonsaetna* took their names from the chief towns of the tribal areas *Lindum* (Lincoln) and *Magnis* (Kenchester) respectively, rather than the name of the tribe, and this also appears to have happened with the Cornovii. The latter's territory included most, if not all, of Cheshire and the hidage figure suggests its boundaries remained largely unaltered as it transmuted into the lands of the *Wrocensaetna*, perhaps later being subsumed into Din Eirth and, finally, Mercia.

The earliest bardic piece to survive from Wales is the poem celebrating the military victories and extensive dominion of Cynan Garwen, king of Din Eirth in the late sixth century.[11] Cynan, father of Selyf ('Serpent in Battles') was the son of Brochfael Ysgithrog ('of the Tusks') who in turn was the son of Cyngen the 'Renowned.' Cyngen's father was Cadell 'Bright-hilt' who had founded the House of Cadell. We shall encounter some of these individuals again in chapter three in the context of the Battle of Chester. A notable aspect of the poem to Cynan is the lack of any mention of a battle against the English. Yet there are plenty of references to campaigns against neighbouring kingdoms within Wales and even against the Britons of Cornwall. It was this internecine warfare that so appalled Gildas. The purpose of his writing was to try and shock the British out of their complacency and limited vision so that they would wake up to the threat posed by the expansionist Anglo-Saxon kingdoms in the east and south-east. To this end he accuses both kings and bishops alike of weakness and wickedness, depicting the Anglo-Saxons as God's punishment for their sins which will only become more severe unless they mend their ways. It is clear from the style and content of his writing that Gildas was aiming to reach an audience that was educated, familiar with Latin and, if not exactly large numerically, then certainly sizeable and influential, including both his fellow clergy and the aristocracy. Society may have become more parochial but it was evidently still very Roman in character and continued the hierarchical nature of the late Roman Empire. This was the situation across the Channel in Gaul as revealed by the letters of Sidonius Apollinaris, Bishop of Auvergne at Clermont Ferrand at the end of the fifth century, which describe a society where bishops were usually recruited from the aristocracy.[12] An example closer to home is Saint Patrick, whose father was a city councillor, possibly at Carlisle.[13] With their background and as the senior representatives of the state religion it was only natural as times became more uncertain that such men increasingly donned the mantle of responsibility for secular affairs as well as spiritual authority. Bishops were city-based and thus looked after and were supported by urban congregations, and so the senior clergy inherited responsibility for maintaining the fabric of urban society.

Alongside evidence for the continuing occupation of some towns (shortly to be described) both documentary sources and archaeology show that many hilltop sites defended in the prehistoric period were recommissioned in the fifth and sixth centuries. This happened not just in Wales, at sites such as Dinas Emrys and Dinorben in Gwynedd or Deganwy in Din Eirth, but also in the West Country.[14] Similarly, towards the end of this period, Ida of Northumbria established his capital within the prehistoric fortress at Bamburgh, endowing it with new and powerful defences.[15] This was a logical and sensible development in uncertain and turbulent times. With no extensive military infrastructure to provide the chance of relief or reinforcement the ideal sites were those that possessed strong defences capable of being held by a small force. The Roman towns which continued in existence also undoubtedly possessed military leaders. A tombstone ploughed up at Wroxeter in 1968 appears to commemorate such a man. The inscription is written in Latin letters but with an Irish spelling and reads CUNORIX MACUS MAQUI COLINE or 'Cunorix (hound-king) son of, son of the Holly'.[16] The epitaph is dated to the latter part of the fifth century and Cunorix is thought to have been a mercenary commander hired by the citizenry to protect the city. Similarly, at the battle of Dyrham in Gloucestershire in 577, the defeated British leaders are described as the 'kings' of Bath, Cirencester and Gloucester (ASC). As regards our own city, one of the leaders of the British forces at the Battle of Chester c.616 is described as '*consul urbis*' or 'Consul of the City.' Admittedly, this reference occurs in Geoffrey of Monmouth's *History of the Kings of Britain* written some 500 years after the event, but he was using early sources which were independent of those available to Bede.[17]

The third phenomenon which had an influence upon settlement patterns in western Britain in this period was the activities of the Celtic Church. This was the 'Age of the Saints'; not only prominent individuals like Patrick, David and Columba but also hundreds of minor 'saints' remembered in place-names and church-dedications. Many of the establishments they founded, or that were founded in their name, were very modest, consisting of an enclosure containing an oratory accompanied by a cross or shrine, the cleric's modest dwelling and a plot of ground cultivated by him. During his lifetime, and even more following his demise, followers chose to be buried nearby.[18] In the sixth century sizeable monastic communities began to appear on the scene and these expanded rapidly with royal patronage and endowments. The larger monasteries had famous schools where, as Bu'Lock put it, 'the civilized inheritance which the Church brought from the classical world could be preserved and developed in the context of Celtic tradition'.[19] Like such establishments elsewhere, they performed a vital role in the intellectual history of Western Europe. Rulers sent their sons to such places to receive their education and even retired there themselves when they were satisfied their heirs were fit to succeed them. The influence of leading churchmen extended further, for they often played a prominent role in court politics. Asaph and Deiniol were the principal monastic leaders in north Wales, the latter's twin foundations at Bangor-on-Menai and Bangor-on-Dee being particularly successful. Former kings of both Gwynedd and Din Eirth numbered among the inhabitants of the monastery at Bangor-on-Dee at the time of the Battle of Chester c.AD 616.

For the first 200 years of the period covered by this book we have only the merest slivers of evidence as to what was happening in Chester. The same situation obtains in many of the major settlements of late Roman Britain. The severance of Britain from the Roman Empire created a situation in which many of the forms of evidence previously available to assess the nature and intensity of activity simply disappeared. The mass production of many articles, including pottery, ceased; the monetary economy collapsed, with coins becoming useless except for the value of the metal of which they were made; and the vast majority of any building work undertaken was carried out using perishable materials. The recognition of the ephemeral remains of such buildings is often only achieved through the undertaking of large-scale area excavation, something rarely possible in modern urban situations. Compounding the situation even further, in those Roman towns and cities which were to become prosperous again many centuries later, the levels potentially containing information relating to this period are usually those which have suffered most damage by subsequent activity.

Fortunately for our purposes, some Roman towns were abandoned well before the Norman Conquest and excavation of their uncluttered interiors has provided an illuminating picture of life in such places during the centuries immediately following the end of Roman rule. An example close to home is Wroxeter, *Viroconium Cornoviorum*, tribal capital of the Cornovii. Here, excavation in the 1960s and 1970s on the site of the town baths revealed a complex sequence of sub-Roman occupation.[20] Not long into the fifth century, maintenance of the baths basilica along traditional lines ceased and, instead, a collection of modest wattle-and-daub structures were erected inside this great aisled hall, which in this phase still retained its roof. At the same time, the external porticoes were dismantled and timber structures erected in their place, one of which contained a large bread oven. Eventually, the roof of the basilica deteriorated to the point where the building was no longer safe to use and so it was dismantled and the supporting columns removed. Despite being a mere shell the basilica continued in use. Earth and the now-redundant roofing slates were used to form pathways and areas of hard standing which in places exhibited considerable wear. As this change coincided with the removal of the structures from the neighbouring portico areas it was suggested that the activities once carried on in them were now transferred to the basilica interior and that it now functioned as a market. A date of 490-550 for the last firing of the bread oven mentioned above was obtained using the remanent magnetism technique.

The final major phase of building commenced around 540 and began with a thorough remodelling of this part of the city. The basilica shell was demolished and its site prepared for the erection of a number of buildings set on slightly elevated platforms made of demolition rubble and materials brought in from other parts of the city. Although most of the new buildings were constructed of timber they were nonetheless substantial. The example designated 'Building 10' was particularly impressive, measuring more than 15 x 30m. Raised on what must have been massive beams laid on the platform, it was competently laid out to a plan harking back to Roman models, consisting of a main block elaborated by a projecting wing or tower at either end of its frontage and a two-columned porch framing its centrally placed entrance. It was certainly capable of rising to two, if not three, storeys in height. Many other buildings, of more modest proportions, were found nearby; the majority seemingly more suited to storage rather than residential purposes. In the neighbouring baths-suite the hypocausts which had long since passed out of use had at least a dozen burials inserted into them. When discovered in the late nineteenth century these were considered to be victims of some imagined sacking of the town in the Dark Ages. In the light of the more recent work, and discoveries in other Roman towns, the suggestion has been made that these belonged to an early Christian cemetery associated with a church or chapel formed out of what had once been the *frigidarium* of the baths. This happened to be on an appropriate alignment east/west and was equipped with a plunge-pool ideal for baptisms. Other buildings of this period were found on neighbouring plots. A variety of building techniques were employed. Some were raised on ground-based beams, others had their main vertical wall-posts set in pits, while yet others were built with clay walls. Modest in size, these seem likely to have been dwellings.

The sequence at Wroxeter demonstrates quite convincingly that town life on an organised basis could continue long after the end of Roman rule. The radical remodelling of the baths site in the mid-sixth century, with its inclusion of an imposing residence and hints of an ecclesiastical presence, points to the existence of an able and strong governing authority. It has also been suggested that this reorganisation came about as a result of the *mortalitas magna* (the Great Death – almost certainly the bubonic plague) which reached Britain in 547 and which counted Maelgwn of Gwynedd among its victims.[21] Some of the buildings erected at this time were rebuilt on three subsequent occasions, suggesting occupation enduring for at least another fifty years. Wroxeter was eventually abandoned at some point in the first half of the seventh century when the area was absorbed into Mercia.

It is likely that in Chester, too, occupation of some form continued unbroken throughout the two centuries following the break with Rome. As was described in chapter one, *Deva* was still an important centre in the closing decades of the fourth century. Its population may well have declined significantly from *c*.AD 350 as a consequence of successive withdrawals of troops and their families, but it is likely that there was still a community of some significance living within the fortress. Common sense alone makes it very unlikely that the entire population dispersed into the surrounding countryside. Certainly, without state salaries and subsidies many people would have suddenly found that they needed an alternative way of earning a living. The bartering of skills and services for food and goods would soon have replaced a monetary economy. Some presumably became subsistence farmers, keeping animals and growing crops perhaps on land rented to them by others who had been farmers for generations. The land around Chester is of variable quality in agricultural terms but would certainly have supported both arable and pastoral farming. The River Dee and the marshes along its estuary provided a rich source of food with its fish and waterfowl. The river also afforded a means of both communication and trade. The fabric of the fortress may soon have begun to deteriorate but it still provided a place of refuge and it is probable that there was at least one church within its walls which would have continued in existence throughout this period. As mentioned in chapter one, there is some evidence for a bishopric based in Chester in the fourth century which also controlled a salt-producing centre near Crewe which lasted into the sixth or seventh century.

The possibility that Chester continued as a place of religious importance is indicated, if obliquely, by the event which marks the city's re-emergence into recorded history at the dawn of the seventh century. This was a synod of the British Church held '*in Urbs Legionis*' and recorded in the *Annales Cambriae* against the year 601 and also by Bede, who describes the Roman site as '*Civitas Legionis*'.[22] It is true that the name *Urbs Legionis* could also refer to Caerleon, but the odds are weighted heavily in favour of Chester because the synod was presided over by Abbot Dinoot, known to have been head of the monastery at Bangor-is-y-Coed (Bangor-on-Dee). The conference was arranged in response to pressure exerted by Augustine of Canterbury (backed by the power of his patron, King Aethelbert of Kent) on British churchmen further south to acknowledge the supremacy of the Roman Church. The matter had remained undecided at an earlier meeting known as the Conference of Augustine's Oak and so a second was organised. Chester had much to commend it as the location for such a meeting. It lay at a nodal point of the largely still functioning Roman road-system approximately the same travelling distance for clergy coming from either the North-West or from Wales and the South-West. It could be reached by sea and one of the principal monasteries of the day lay near at hand. There is also the underlying implication that it could accommodate and cater for a sizeable number of clergy and also provide a suitable venue for the actual assembly. It is tempting to speculate that this was the putative church mentioned above; or could it perhaps have been the great basilical hall of the old legionary *principia*, the centuries-old focus of administration and justice in the city? The leaders of the British Church decided how to receive Augustine's proposals and, on the advice of a local hermit, devised a test of Augustine's humility. This he failed and seven bishops then went to see Augustine to deliver the rejection of his proposals. Perhaps one of these men was Bishop of Chester. Bede, writing from a pro-English and pro-Augustinian point of view, saw the slaughter of monks at the Battle of Chester a few years later as divine punishment meted out to the British churchmen for their obstinacy at the synod.

While one can speculate freely about the unbroken occupation of Chester throughout the sub-Roman period, conclusive proof, in the form of archaeological evidence, continues to be very elusive. However, a few clues have emerged in recent years. One such has come from analysing the records of the hurried investigations of the fortress baths conducted in the 1960s prior to publication (see *2*).[23] Much of the eastern half of this great complex was occupied by a suite of three massive bathing-halls, each 12m wide and at least 22m long, arranged in a north–south progression of increasing temperature from cold (*frigidarium*), through warm (*tepidarium*) to hot (*caldarium*). These vast chambers had walls over a metre thick and they were covered by concrete barrel-vaults. One small area at the east end of the *tepidarium* was examined during a temporary halt in the site clearance work. Here, the hypocaust and the floor above it had survived completely intact. The final surfacing of the latter consisted of large slabs of slate and over these was a layer of dark grey/almost black earth about 300mm thick (*colour plate 1*). This in its turn was sealed by a mass of broken tile and fragmented concrete and plaster representing the collapsed roofing-vault and its external cladding. The dark earth had clearly formed during the time between the end of the chamber's use for bathing and the eventual collapse of its roof. That this had been a lengthy interval is obvious from the substantial accumulation of earth on its floor, and in this connection it is worth noting that the roofing vaults of the fortress baths at Caerleon are thought to have survived until the twelfth century.[24]

Sadly, there was not time to investigate the earth layer in any detail, but the records shed some light on the range of materials within it. These included fragments of plaster presumably derived from the gradual decay of the lining of the walls and ceiling along with fragments of animal bone and small areas of charcoal. It is conceivable that the accumulation of this deposit was caused entirely by natural processes such as colonisation by flora and the ingress of wind-blown material through broken windows, supplemented by the results of animal, and especially bird and bat, activity; we are all only too aware, for example, of the considerable volume of material which can result from pigeon infestation! Then again, some, or even the majority, of it may have been the consequence of human occupation or use. Certainly, although redundant as far as its original function was concerned, the size and especially the robustness of the baths complex would have rendered it suitable for a variety of purposes in the early post-Roman period. More so than many of the other, less substantial, buildings in the fortress which, without constant care and maintenance, would soon have become unusable. Some parts of the baths may have been turned into residential accommodation, others given over to storage, with yet others actually continuing to be used for bathing or washing, albeit probably with unheated water. Thus, different elements of this vast complex may have had divergent and contrasting histories in the fifth and sixth centuries. Much of the basilical-style exercise hall occupying the north side of the complex, as large as the nave of the cathedral, was revealed by redevelopment work in the 1860s. Here, too, the evidence, in this case the discovery of the main supporting columns lying where they had fallen, speaks of gradual decay and ultimate collapse rather than deliberate demolition. The same situation appears to have prevailed in the equally vast basilical hall of the headquarters building, whose tumbled columns were found in the 1890s.[25]

5 Eastern fortress wall showing fracturing of facing-blocks caused by outwards collapse in early medieval period. St John Street 1989

Elsewhere in the fortress, and also in the civil settlement around it, evidence of activity in this period is extremely scarce. Some idea of the state of the fortress defences is provided by the results of an excavation on a section of the city wall south of the Eastgate in 1989, an opportunity afforded by the demolition of the former Public Library building in St John Street. Usually, where the medieval and Roman defensive circuits coincide the town wall sits almost directly atop the fortress wall, but here the medieval wall stands several metres back from the Roman masonry and follows an alignment which diverges from it increasingly to the south. The excavation revealed that a long stretch of the fortress wall had gradually tilted forwards, the pressure causing the front edges of the blocks in the lower courses to fracture and sheer off (5).[26] Eventually, the point was reached where the masonry collapsed, followed closely by a proportion of the rampart which it had revetted. The resultant low mound of rubble and soil completely obscured the precise line of the wall. A ditch of modest proportions was cut into this subsequently and would seem to be associated with some form of refurbishment of the defences. This happened long after the collapse but well before the construction of the town wall and might have been connected with the refortification of Chester in the opening years of the tenth century. Other parts of the fortress wall also eventually fell outwards, as can be seen in the long stretch between the steps giving access from Frodsham Street and the north-east angle. There, however, the process was far slower, allowing sufficient time for the external ground level to rise and support the tilting wall. The sector south of the Eastgate may well have had an inherent weakness. Whereas elsewhere on the Roman defences the masonry wall was simply added to the front of the earlier rampart, in this sector the rampart was actually cut back to receive it, suggesting that here the berm was narrower than usual. Later re-cuttings may have reduced the gap between the edge of the ditch and the front of the wall still further, weakening the foundation and creating structural instability.

By the time of the synod of c.601, Chester probably had a rather mixed appearance. For the most part, the defences would still have been in relatively good condition, although certain sections may already have begun to collapse. The gate-houses would certainly have looked little different from a couple of centuries earlier. We know that the east gate, for example, was still substantially intact as late as the thirteenth century when a new gate structure was added to its frontage and there is no reason for thinking the other three gates fared any less well.[27] Most of the major fortress buildings such as the baths, the *principia*, the commandant's residence and the Elliptical Building would still have been standing and perhaps habitable in part. The barrack buildings on the other hand, unless the subject of constant maintenance, would have fallen into disrepair and significant collapse some time earlier. Smaller habitations could have arisen in their stead, however, built of stone robbed from the remainder or from more perishable materials. In the *canabae* it seems safe to assume that major structures such as the Watergate Baths and the amphitheatre were still largely intact, while modest dwellings presumably still existed on the sites of the earlier densely packed commercial premises. Medieval chroniclers believed that the collegiate church of St John the Baptist, situated just beyond the amphitheatre outside the south-east angle of the fortress, was founded about 689 by King Ethelred and Bishop Wilfrid.[28] Although impossible to prove, this would fit into the pattern of new church foundations following the conversion of Mercia in the middle of the seventh century. The choice of location is fascinating on a number of counts. If, as amphitheatres were the usual venues for public excecutions, Christians were put to death here during one of the periodic persecutions that occurred throughout the Roman Empire in the third century then the place may well have had an association with Christian martyrs which any new foundation would have been keen to exploit. This association could have found expression in the building of some form of martyrial shrine in the late Roman period, like those found in a number of amphitheatres on the continent.[29] There is also the possibility that St John's was built in this extramural location for the more prosaic reason that, as discussed in chapter one, there was already a church inside the fortress, most probably on the site of the later St Werburgh's.

During the Roman period several civil settlements grew up within a few kilometres of the fortress and its *canabae*, the most important of which lay at Heronbridge, lining Watling Street 1.5km to the south of *Deva* and standing beside the River Dee (see *4*). Recent excavations here have demonstrated that, while occupation continued down to the end of the fourth century, its buildings were in ruins well before the opening years of the seventh century. Less than 1km further to the south lies the village of Eccleston, which has a place-name potentially very significant for our period. It is a hybrid formed from the Primitive Welsh version of the Modern Welsh *eglwys*/Old English *ecles*, both derivations from the Latin *ecclesia* ('congregation' or 'church') and the Old English -*tun*. Thus the name Eccleston is understood to denote a 'church-settlement' or 'Christian-community' which was encountered by the first English settlers.[30] It seems very likely, therefore, that at some time during the period 400–600 the community living at Heronbridge decided, for reason or reasons unknown, to relocate itself a short distance to the south. They were not to know that their former home was to be the site of one of the most dramatic events of the seventh century and one that, ultimately, led to the creation of the England and Wales we know today.

A RUDE AWAKENING: THE COMING OF THE ENGLISH

HISTORY

The decades either side of AD 600 were a time of rapid swings in fortune for many of the kingdoms in Britain, both English and British (for map showing location of kingdoms see 6). It was also a period in which loyalties and alliances changed swiftly while treachery was commonplace on both sides and at every turn. Around 580, in an attempt to eradicate the expanding Anglian kingdom of Bernicia (northern Northumbria), which at that time was ruled by Theodric, son of Ida, the first Bernician king, the North British princes launched a series of successful counter-attacks. Chief amongst these princes were three descendants of the prestigious house of Coel: Morcant, Guallaug and Urien. Guallaug was king of Elmet, centred on south-west Yorkshire, and Urien was ruler of Rheged, the great north-western kingdom south of the Solway. Chapter 63 of the *Historia Brittonum* gives an account of this campaign, possibly written by Urien's son Rhun:

> Urien shut them (the Bernicians) up three days and three nights in the island of Metcaud (Lindisfarne), and while he was on an expedition he was murdered, at the instance of Morcant, out of envy, because in him above all the kings was the greatest skill in the renewing of battle.

The murder of Urien was remembered by later Welsh poets as a disaster for the northern kingdoms, marking the retreat of British power to Strathclyde and North Wales. Urien's son, Owein, also perished continuing the fight, but a second son, Rhun, became a monk and historian. He made the extracts from a *Book of St Germanus* which, with his own memoranda, formed the basis of the *Northern*

Chronicle and later the *Historia Brittonum* of Nennius. He survived long enough to see his grand-daughter marry a Northumbrian prince. With Rheged's power failing, North Wales became the centre of opposition to Anglian expansion. The two principal kingdoms there were Gwynedd and Din Eirth (later known as Powys), the latter then at its greatest extent and encompassing the lands between the Rivers Conwy and Dee. St Deiniol, another descendant of Coel Hen, was very active in the area and before his death in 584 he had founded two great monasteries, at Bangor-on-Menai in Gwynedd and Bangor-is-y-Coed (Bangor-on-Dee) in Powys. Bede describes the monastery at Bangor-on-Dee as self-supporting and divided into seven sections, each headed by a learned scholar and containing more than three hundred monks. It was commonplace at this time for ageing warriors and even rulers to retire to such places. Two former kings are mentioned, both of whom were to feature in the Battle of Chester (fought *c.* 616): Iago ap Beli, formerly King of Gwynedd, and Brochfael Ysgithrog, one-time King of Din Eirth of the House of Cadell. They had entrusted their realms to men who were well known not just for valour but also for their learning and culture. Cynan Garwen of Din Eirth was a patron of poets such as Taliesin, a refugee from the north, while Cadvan of Gwynedd is described in his epitaph, preserved in a church near Aberffraw on Anglesey, as '*rex sapientissimus, opinatissimus omnium regum*' ('the wisest and most renowned of all kings').[1] As the main centres of learning and culture, it was also to the monasteries that the male children of the nobility were sent to receive their education.

The Bernicians had narrowly escaped destruction at the hands of Urien, but under their new king, Aethelric, another son of Ida, they recovered and began to acquire new territory. In 588 Aethelric absorbed the neighbouring kingdom of Deira into his realm when its leader, Aelle, died; an event possibly engineered by Aethelric himself. To bolster the legitimacy of his claim on Deira, Aethelric arranged a marriage between Acha, Aelle's daughter, and his own son and heir Aethelfrith. Edwin, the infant brother of Aelle, was spirited away to safety by Deiran loyalists. They found sanctuary in the lands of the Britons opposing Aethelric and eventually the three-year-old Deiran heir came under the protection of Cadvan of Gwynedd. Here he grew up as foster-brother to the king's son Cadwallon. In keeping with the spirit of the times, these two would later become deadly rivals. Aethelfrith succeeded to the Northumbrian throne in 593 and soon began to outdo his father in military prowess. Taking pride in this local, if pagan, hero Bede tells us that he:

> … ravaged the Britons more than all the great men of the English … [and] conquered more territories … either making them tributary or driving out the inhabitants.

> (H.E. i.34)

6 The British and Anglo-Saxon kingdoms c.AD 600 (British kingdoms underlined)

In 603 Aethelfrith achieved what was arguably his greatest victory at the Battle of Degsaetan, when he defeated a large army assembled by Aedan mac Gabrain, King of the Dalriadic Scots, the recently established kingdom of Irish settlers in Argyll, aided by warriors from Ulster and probably the North Britons. The contest was fierce, both Aethelfrith's brother Theodbald and the Ulster king Maeluma perished, but the result left Aethelfrith in complete control of the upper Tweed valley and, perhaps more importantly, Carlisle and the lands around it. As we saw in the preceding chapter, it is at this point that Chester re-emerges into the historical record as the probable venue for the second conference with Augustine.

As Edwin grew up, his resentment at his disinheritance grew apace. He also realised with every year that passed that he ran an increasing risk of assassination by Aethelfrith's agents. He must also have been acutely aware that his host's hospitality was based solely on his own usefulness as a pawn in the game of alliances. In other words, 'my enemy's enemy is my friend.' Apart from flight even further afield, pursuing the recovery of Deira was the only option open to Edwin. Aethelfrith's strength was such that he could only be toppled by a powerful alliance and it was to this that Edwin directed his efforts in the decade following the failure of Augustine's mission. His foster-father Cadvan would help and so, too, would Din Eirth as it was threatened more immediately by Northumbrian expansion. Edwin also planned to enlist the assistance of English as well as British rulers. He took as his wife Quenburga, daughter of Ceorl, a Mercian sub-king, thus ensuring the support of her kinsmen. Next he travelled to the East Anglian court of Raedwald, a powerful and devious monarch. It is of course Raedwald who is thought to have been interred in the Sutton Hoo ship-burial. Following the death of Ethelbert, Raedwald cast aside his nominal allegiance to the Kentish royal house. The arrival of Edwin at his court intensified Raedwald's ambitions.

Edwin's activities were detected by Aethelfrith, who decided to launch a pre-emptive strike before the hostile alliance could be completed. He sent ambassadors to Raedwald to try to persuade him to refuse Edwin's overtures and either arrange his death or at the very least his expulsion from court. Simultaneously, Aethelfrith himself set forth with a great army in 616 with the aim of destroying the forces of the British kingdoms in North Wales before they could combine with those of Mercia.[2] Undoubtedly making use of the Roman road system, Aethelfrith swept down into Cheshire with such speed that the British were taken by surprise and could only muster a hastily assembled force to oppose him. This consisted essentially of the army of Din Eirth led by Selyf, son of Cynan, supported by a small contingent from eastern Gwynedd under Cadwal Crisban of Rhos. The situation was so desperate that the British had to depend on a contingent of monks from the monastery at Bangor-on-Dee to hold the flanks. In this period it was commonplace for warriors, the nobility and even kings to retire to such establishments. Thus, present in the contingent were Selyf's grandfather Brochfael, once king of Din Eirth, and Iago ap Beli, a former king of Gwynedd. Proficient warriors these men may once have been, but they had not raised their swords in anger for many a long year. This became all too apparent when Aethelfrith launched his main attack against this weakest component in the British force.

Bede's account of the battle runs as follows:

> For later on [after the second synod with Augustine], that very powerful king of the English Aethelfrith, whom we have already spoken of, collected a great army against the city of the legions (*Civitas Legionis*), which is called Legacaestir by the English, and more correctly Caerlegion by the Britons, and made a great slaughter of that nation of heretics. When he was about to give battle and saw their priests who had assembled to pray to God on behalf of the soldiers taking part in the fight, standing apart in a safer place, he asked who they were and for what purpose they had gathered there. Most of them were from the monastery of Bangor, where there was said to be so great a number of monks that, when it was divided into seven parts with superiors over each, no division contained less than 300 monks, all of whom were accustomed to live by the labour of their hands. After a three-days' fast, most of these had come to the battle in order to pray for the others. They had a guard named Brocmail, whose duty it was to protect them from the swords of the barbarians while they were praying. When Aethelfrith heard why they had come he said 'If they are praying to their God against us, then, even if they do not bear arms they are fighting against us, assailing us as they do with prayers for our defeat.' He therefore directed his first attack against them, and then destroyed the rest of the accursed army, not without heavy loss to his own forces. It is said that of the monks who had come to pray about twelve hundred perished in this battle, and only fifty escaped by flight. Brochmail and his men took to their heels at the first assault, leaving those whom they should have protected unarmed and exposed to the sword-strokes of the enemy. Thus, long after his death, was fulfilled Bishop Augustine's prophecy that the faithless Britons, who had rejected the offer of eternal salvation, would incur the punishment of temporal destruction.
>
> (H.E. ii.2)

According to the *Welsh Annals* Selyf, Cadwal and Iago all perished along with hundreds of others (*sub anno* 613). Soundly beaten, the Britons fled the battlefield. Bede took great pleasure in portraying the British defeat as divine punishment for the Celtic Church's refusal to submit to Augustine's authority. The northern rescension of the *Anglo-Saxon Chronicle* gives the figure of monks killed as 200 but repeats the figure of 50 escapees (*sub anno* 605).

Bede continues the story a few chapters later where he describes how Raedwald vacillated for some time about which side to support. We are told that Raedwald eventually decided in favour of Aethelfrith, no doubt on hearing of the latter's victory at Chester, or at least his march towards it, and agreed either to murder Edwin or hand him over to his enemies. However, the queen interceded on Edwin's behalf and apparently persuaded Raedwald that it would be unworthy for a great king to betray a guest:

> In brief, the king did as she advised, and not only refused to surrender the exiled prince but assisted him to recover his kingdom. As soon as the envoys had gone home, he raised a great army to make war on Ethelfrid and allowing him no time to summon his full strength, encountered him with superior forces and killed him. In this battle, which was fought in Mercian territory on the east bank of the River Idle, Raegenhere, son of Raedwald, also met his death. So Edwin ... succeeded to his throne.
>
> (H.E. ii.12)

A rather different account of these events is given in Geoffrey of Monmouth's *History of the Kings of Britain* and Reginald of Durham's *Life of Oswald*, both of whom drew on early sources independent of Bede. They also give an indication of what happened in the immediate aftermath of the battle:

> When Ethelbert, the King of the men of Kent, saw that the Britons were refusing to accept the authority of Augustine and were scorning his preaching, he bore it very ill. He stirred up Ethelfrid, King of the Northumbrians, and a number of other petty kings of the Saxons. A huge army was assembled and ordered to march to the city of Bangor and destroy Abbot Dinoot and the other churchmen who had scorned Augustine. They accepted Ethelbert's orders, collected an enormous army together and set out for the land of the Britons. They came to Chester, where Brochmail, who was in command of that city, awaited their coming. A great number of monks and hermits from all the different territories of the Britons, and especially from the city of Bangor, had sought refuge in Chester, so that they could pray there for the people's safety. Armies were drawn up on both sides, and Ethelfrid, King of the Northumbrians, joined battle with Brochmail. Brochmail stood firm against him, although his force was smaller. In the end, however, Brochmail abandoned the city and fled, but only after inflicting enormous losses on the enemy. When Ethelfrid occupied the city and discovered the reason why these monks whom I have mentioned had come there, he immediately let his soldiery loose against them. That same day twelve hundred monks won the crown of martyrdom and assured themselves of a seat in heaven. After this, the Saxon tyrant marched to the town of Bangor. When they heard of his mad frenzy, the leaders of the Britons came from all directions to oppose him: Blederic, Duke of Cornwall; Margadud, King of the Demetae; and Cadvan of the Venedoti. Battle was joined. They wounded Ethelfrid and forced him to flee. They killed so many of his army that some ten thousand and sixty-six died that day. On the side of the Britons there died Blederic, Duke

of Cornwall, who commanded the others in these wars. All the princes of the Britons then assembled in the city of Chester and agreed unanimously that they should make Cadvan their King and that under his command they should cross the Humber in pursuit of Ethelfrid. Once Cadvan had been crowned King of the realm, these princes gathered from all sides and crossed the Humber. The moment that this news reached Ethelfrid, he came to an understanding with all the kings of the Saxons and then marched out to meet Cadvan. Just as they were in the act of drawing up their battle-squadrons on both sides, their friends arrived and made peace between them. The agreement they came to was that Ethelfrid should hold the part of Britain which lay beyond the Humber, and Cadvan the part on this side.

(H.K.B xi.13–xii.1)

After this both the chronology and relationships become very confused. Edwin is made out to be a son of Ethelfrid and both Aurelius Ambrosianus and Arthur are introduced into the story along with a variety of other, even more exotic, personages.

Leaving aside the obvious embroideries by Geoffrey of Monmouth, a number of common threads emerge from the various accounts despite the minor inconsistencies. Aethelfrith clearly took advantage of Edwin's absence at Raedwald's court to launch his attack. His descent from Bamburgh was so rapid it obviously took the British by surprise. Their response was the only one possible in the circumstances: they mustered what forces they could to prevent, or at least delay, his striking deep into North Wales, and these were accompanied by a sizeable contingent of unarmed monks who had come to add the power of prayer. The initial encounter took place in or close by the old fortress site, Aethelfrith's forces were victorious and the monks were slaughtered. An important point to note is the emphasis on the losses sustained by the Northumbrians. From the sources used by Geoffrey of Monmouth it would appear that there were two major battles: the first at Chester itself, and the second at the monastery at Bangor-is-y-Coed. This is supported by the Welsh Triads where the Battle of Chester is referred to in triad 60 as *Gueith Perllan Vangor*, 'the Action of Bangor Orchard.' Given the part played by monks from that establishment in the battle at Chester it would have been a natural target for Aethelfrith's forces in the wake of the first engagement. Whether or not this second battle actually occurred it is clear that Aethelfrith was either unwilling or unable to maintain his army at Chester for very long. The loss of men had been considerable, the supply lines were probably over-extended, and the British forces, led by Cadvan of Gwynedd, were re-grouping. Furthermore, he had probably heard of Raedwald's decision to support Edwin, something no doubt prompted by news of the losses suffered by the Northumbrians rather than by any crisis of conscience. Aethelfrith had no choice but to withdraw and it would have made sense to have done so before winter set in. The Northumbrian line of retreat apparently took them through the southern Pennines. Here they were probably harassed by the Mercian warriors of Edwin's father-in-law Ceorl before finally being set upon and crushed by Raedwald's army at Bawtry, on the Nottinghamshire/South Yorkshire border. After living 28 of his 31 years of life in exile, constantly in fear for his life, Edwin returned in triumph to Northumbria as its king. One might have thought that this would have resulted in a period of peace for Chester and the surrounding region but, as we shall see at the beginning of chapter four, this was not to be.

From the account given above it can be seen that in the early seventh century the people living in Chester suddenly found themselves on the fault-line of conflict between Anglian Northumbria on the one side and the British kingdoms of North Wales, usually aided by the growing power of English Mercia, on the other. Chester became a frontier town and in fact this was to be its role for most of the next 350 years, although the identity and nationality of the opposing powers were to change many times, as did the intensity of hostility. Armies of both sides crossed our region periodically in the first half of the seventh century and occasionally, as with the battles at Chester and Oswestry, major and decisive engagements occurred nearby. The sources record that Northumbria was ravaged on several occasions when the other side was in the ascendant. The Northumbrians presumably behaved in a similar fashion when they descended on what is now Cheshire. Having grown up as an exile in Gwynedd, Edwin would have been well acquainted with North Wales and when he returned as its would-be conqueror in the early 630s it is possible that he established his forward base at Chester. As Aethelfrith had demonstrated by the speed of his advance some years before, it was well served by the surviving Roman road network and would also have afforded a secure anchorage for a fleet supporting his advance along the North Wales coast and his seizure of the Isle of Man.

Although it was the Northumbrians who were responsible for weakening Din Eirth's hold on Cheshire and opening the way for English settlement in the county, this was actually achieved in a rather more peaceable fashion as far as one can judge by Anglians from the Midlands. This would have taken place in the context of the alliance, or series of alliances, between the rulers of North Wales and Mercia, initiated, ironically, by Edwin. In a period when every ruler engaged in playing off one rival against another, one can well imagine that the kings of North Wales would have been content to have Mercians settling in eastern Powys to act as a buffer between themselves and the greater threat posed by Northumbria. This is not to say that the Welsh rulers allowed the Mercians to settle in Cheshire. Mercia, as we have seen, had become a formidable military power in its own right and the kings of Powys and Gwynedd would have been ill advised to try to oppose Mercian settlement. Rather, they merely allowed it to happen unopposed, coming to an accommodation with Mercia and content that the two English kingdoms would carry on fighting each other instead of trying to take more of the British West. The agreement with Mercia may have resulted in the definition of an agreed boundary between their respective territories. Major natural features, especially rivers, were frequently chosen as boundaries. They were easily and clearly recognisable by both parties, thus eliminating the possibility of disputes, and did away with the need for large-scale construction work. Of course, where there was no convenient natural feature some form of artifical boundary would have been needed. Some years ago, Dodgson drew attention to the fact that the River Gowy, about 8km east of Chester, was once called the Tarvin, from which the nearby village took its name.[3] Tarvin comes from the Welsh *terfyn,* itself derived from the Latin *terminum,* a boundary. He suggested this as the line of an early, perhaps the earliest, boundary between Mercia and Din Eirth. Its continuation southwards perhaps indicated by the place-name Macefn, near Malpas (*maes-y-ffin* = 'the field at the boundary'). By the end of the seventh century, any such boundary had in all probability been moved westwards. Welsh sources refer to a Mercian frontier at Pulford and although we do not know its date it would fit best into the period around AD 700. Thus, there may have been a series of precursors to that most famous, and most substantial, of Anglo-Saxon boundary markers, Offa's Dyke.

ARCHAEOLOGY

The Battle of Chester

Until very recently little else could be said about the actual battle. Locating the precise site of any battlefield is notoriously difficult. In many engagements the action ranged over a wide area. The final resting-place of those who fell is also rarely discovered. It is easy to understand therefore why not one single battlefield site of the early Anglo-Saxon period in England has been found; that is, not until 2004. As described in chapter one, in addition to the town which grew up around the legionary fortress at Chester there was another sizeable Roman settlement only 1.5km to the south at Heronbridge, straddling Watling Street close beside the River Dee (see *4*). Nothing of the Roman settlement can be seen today but in the fields between Eaton Road, Watling Street's successor, and the river, the remains of an embanked, curvilinear enclosure some six hectares in size are discernible. The line of this earthwork runs parallel with Eaton Road for some 300m before curving round towards the river, sharply at the south end and more gently at the north (*7, 8* and *colour plates 2* and *3*).

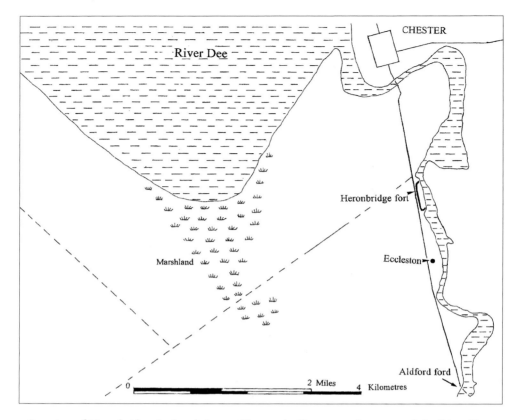

7 Location of Heronbridge site in relation to Chester, the Roman road-system and the River Dee

The discovery that this overlay a Roman settlement was made in 1929 by W.J. Williams (also known as 'Walrus' Williams on account of his prominent moustache), an active member of the Chester Archaeological Society, who found large quantities of Roman pottery and traces of walls whilst searching for the precise line of Watling Street. Formal excavations followed in 1930-31 and were directed by James Petch of Manchester University. These investigated a group of stone buildings on the east side of Watling Street at a spot which we now know lay a little to the north of the heart of the settlement (9).[4]

A surprising discovery made during the course of this work was a group of inhumation burials inserted into the ruins of the buildings and lying just inside the earthwork enclosure. A few of these appeared to be single burials; in one case the body had been placed directly on top of the remains of a Roman wall. The majority however apparently occurred in a mass burial (9 & 10). Approximately 20 skeletons were fully or partially excavated in two groups and there were signs that many more lay in the area outside the excavation. The area between them

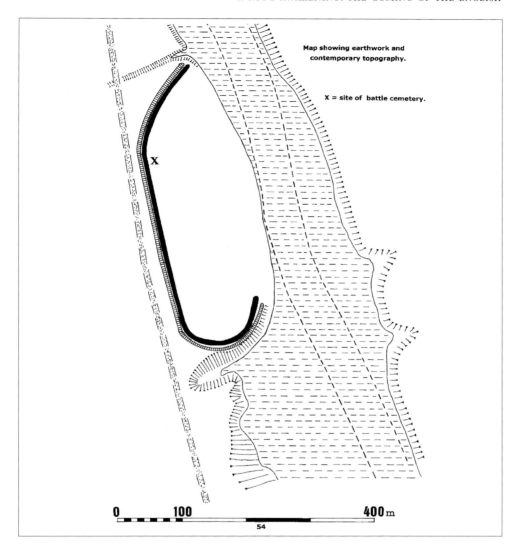

Map showing earthwork and
contemporary topography.

X = site of battle cemetery.

0   100   400 m

54

8 Heronbridge. Plan of seventh-century fort in relation to surrounding topography. Note greater width of river in antiquity. Narrower channel marked in centre of river is that which exists today

was not investigated so it is quite possible that they all belonged to a single mass grave. The bodies had been laid close together in north–south rows lying on their back or side and with the head at the west end. Analysis of the skulls carried out soon afterwards indicated that they were all male, the majority lying in the age-range 20-45, with a high percentage displaying clear evidence of a violent death in the form of blade cuts to the top of the skull.[5] There were no accompanying grave-goods.

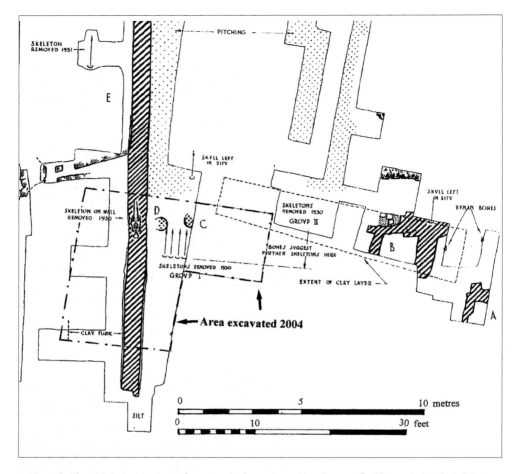

9 Heronbridge. Main excavation of 1930-31 and area investigated 2004. © *Chester Archaeological Society*

The obvious conclusion to be drawn was that they were casualties from a battle which, according to his interpretation of the site's chronology, the excavator placed in the second or third century. A number of sections were cut through the neighbouring earthwork around the same time and these revealed that the low bank which exists today is the remnant of what had once been a formidable set of defences. It was discovered that the material to form the bank had been obtained by digging a ditch into the solid clay which forms the subsoil here. The ditch was V-shaped, about 5.5m wide and 3m deep, which would have provided sufficient material to form a rampart 2.5m in height and about 4.5m wide. In some sections there were hints that the bank had originally been revetted at the front with a drystone wall formed of re-used Roman masonry, but this was far from certain.

10 Heronbridge. Skeletons uncovered during the 1930–31 excavation. © *Chester Archaeological Society*

11 Heronbridge. 1930–31 trench showing side-wall of Roman building. Note large re-used stone block. © *Chester Archaeological Society*

12 Heronbridge 2004. Re-excavation of part of 1930-1 trench showing same length of wall

Excavations resumed at Heronbridge after the War, again carried out by the Chester Archaeological Society, continuing intermittently until 1967.[6] Although these did not re-examine the 'battle cemetery,' evidence was soon obtained that suggested it was almost certainly later than the Roman period. In an article published in 1951, the late Graham Webster speculated that the Battle of Chester had been fought in the Heronbridge area and that the burials derived from this encounter.[7] Of course, in the absence of grave-goods or the availability of scientific dating techniques, his hypothesis could not be tested. This same lack of conclusive evidence meant that later writers could put forward dates for the burials as far apart as the sixth and seventeenth centuries alongside an equally broad chronological range for the earthwork; the latter viewed in some quarters as an early monastic enclosure[8] and in others as a Civil War period redoubt associated with the 1644 siege of Chester.[9] Attempts were made in the 1980s to locate the skeletons removed from the site in the 1930s with a view to subjecting them to radiocarbon dating but, unfortunately, they could not be found and it seems they had probably been destroyed during the bombing of Manchester in World War II.

The age of both burials and fortification was high on the list of research priorities in a new programme of investigation planned and designed by the writer in conjunction with the Chester Archaeolgical Society for the beginning

13 Heronbridge 2004. Area excavated immediately adjacent to 1930-1 trench showing rubble derived from frontal revetment of seventh-century fort rampart

of the new millennium. Tackling the 'battle cemetery' was left until the third season of work in the summer of 2004. The site of the 1930s excavation was re-located and the portion where the northern group of burials had been found was re-excavated (*9*, *12*, *13* & *14*).[10] A continuation of the row of burials found previously was discovered and two skeletons both male, one in his early twenties and the other in his forties, were extracted for radiocarbon dating (*colour plates 4, 5* & *6*). There was a resigned expectation that the burials would turn out to belong to the period of the English Civil War, although there was also a quiet hope that they would turn out to be seventh century. In the event, the results confirmed with a degree of accuracy beyond expectation that the cemetery did indeed date to the time of the Battle of Chester.

The sample from the skeleton of the older man gave a date in the range AD 430-640 at 95% Confidence and AD 530-620 at 59% Confidence (SUERC 3769). The results for the sample from the younger man's skeleton were a date in the range AD 530-660 at 95% Confidence and AD 595-645 at 52% Confidence (SUERC 3770). The excavation of 2004 also yielded further information about the nature of the mass burial. Not only was a continuation of the row of burials found in 1930-31 revealed but also two other rows to the east. Each row of burials overlapped that to its west to the extent that the heads of the individuals in one row lay above the knees of their neighbours. The westernmost row appeared to

14 Heronbridge 2004. Area excavated beside 1930–31 trench. Re-used Roman tombstones amongst rubble derived from frontal revetment of seventh-century fort rampart

be the final line of burials on that side of the mass grave as there were no other bodies overlying them. As before, there was a total absence of grave-goods or associated objects. Within the modest area measuring 3 x 2.5m examined, there was a minimum of 14 individuals along with the heads of the next row of bodies to the west which continued beyond the area of excavation. The distribution of the burials found previously suggests a mass grave with overall dimensions of approximately 5 x 14m which, extrapolating from the density of burials seen in 2004, would be sufficient to contain at least 120 bodies.

That the battle took place in the vicinity of Chester is understandable given that it stood on the shortest route into North Wales and possessed the lowest crossing of the Dee (see *7*). The deciding factor was presumably the speed with which the hastily assembled British force advanced to meet the oncoming Northumbrians. One can only speculate as to why the battle took place at the particular location of Heronbridge. Chester itself might still have been a place of some importance, if not wealth, in this period. Its population may have fled before the advancing Northumbrian horde or have stayed put and determined to resist as Geoffrey of Monmouth's sources imply. To Aethelfrith, its capture would have been of secondary importance, at least at this stage, because his main objective was the destruction of Edwin and the military strength of the British kingdoms in North Wales. He would not have wanted to have become embroiled in a protracted siege something which Anglo-Saxon armies studiously avoided nor would he have wanted his army's manoeuvrability impeded by setting up camp within the fortress ruins. Had he been more successful, Chester's access to the Irish Sea and its port facilities would have proved most useful, as they did to his successor. Both sides would have wanted battle to take place in open country. Opposing Aethelfrith as he tried to cross the Dee would have been the most likely British strategy, assuming they could get there in time. The old Roman bridge below the fortress was most probably still standing and usable. However, Aethelfrith might have decided to avoid this if it or the south bank was guarded by the local British in strength, for he needed to keep his army intact ready for the main fight. Alternatively, if he was really well informed, he may have made a show of advancing towards the bridge at Chester while sending his main force to cross further upstream. Aldford, where Watling Street crossed the Dee 6km south of Chester, would have been the obvious choice for any British force in the Handbridge/Heronbridge area which would thus have been outflanked and trapped in a pincer movement. There is also a tradition of a ford at the north end of the Heronbridge site itself – the so-called 'Claverton ford' – though its existence has still to be proven.[11] Whether their crossing was opposed or whether the Northumbrians managed to cross safely and make camp for a while before battle was enjoined are moot points, for we now know that some of the fiercest fighting, and very possibly the main part of the battle, took place at Heronbridge itself.

The two skeletons removed for dating in 2004 lay at the north end of the westernmost row of burials. The others belonging to this row lying within the trench were excavated merely to the point where the greater part of the skull could be inspected. It was quite apparent from even a superficial inspection that most of these individuals had sustained head injuries like those seen on the examples excavated in the 1930s (e.g. *colour plate 6*). Further detail was provided by the paleo-pathologist's report. This made for rather grisly reading, as both men had sustained numerous injuries. The younger man had suffered five cranial weapon injuries, four of which would have been fatal in themselves (*colour plate 8*). It was possible to reconstruct the sequence in which the blows had been struck. The first was a blade cut through the centre of the skull, probably inflicted by someone standing to the right of the victim. The cut was a severe, vertical blow causing a wide rift in the top of the skull and splitting it in two through the emanating fracture lines. Another blow, caused by a fine bladed weapon such as a sword, sliced off the very back of the skull (*colour plate 9*) while two others, inflicted again from the right of the victim, had cut into the forehead. The fifth, and probably the final, injury was a cut to the right cheek-bone inflicted by a weapon with a very fine blade (*colour plate 10*).

The older man had sustained four cranial injuries, all blade cuts to the top of the skull (*colour plate 11*). Three of these could be sequenced on the basis of the associated fracture lines. The first sliced across the right side of the head with the second perpendicular to it creating a cross or X-shape. Both of these blows had been inflicted by someone standing in front and to the right of the victim. The third blow, by contrast, had been struck by an opponent standing to the left front. It was also less well defined and the victim may already have been collapsing to the ground. The fourth injury, impossible to sequence, was a shallow cut just behind the right ear. The upper edge was clearly defined by a relatively deep horizontal line from which vertical lines of varying length ran downwards, almost in a comb-like manner but irregularly spaced (*colour plate 12*). This injury may have been caused by a glancing blow from a weapon with a worn and/or damaged blade. It is just conceivable, although considered unlikely in the paleo-pathologist's report, that this was caused by the practice of removing ears as trophies soon after the battle.[12] Even this was not the totality of the injuries suffered by this man. The second lumbar vertebra had been penetrated by a stab wound from the front, the tip of what was evidently a fine-bladed weapon such as a narrow sword or long dagger cutting through the vertebra into the intervertebral disc. The blow had come from the right front of the victim cutting through the lower abdomen to the spine. Finally, the thumb on his right hand exhibited a shallow and unhealed cut, probably sustained in trying to defend himself against multiple attackers (*colour plate 13*).

Clearly both men had been in the very thick of the fighting and appear, judging by the number and type of injuries, to have found themselves outnumbered and to have been struck down by opponents who were evidently under the influence of the 'red mist' of battle. It was suggested in the analysis of the skeletons extracted in the 1930s that the cranial injuries may have been inflicted by sword-wielding cavalry. While the more recent study also concluded that swords were the most likely weapon it is now thought more probable that the men who were using them were fighting on foot, for otherwise the blows with which they struck down their opponents would have been less vertical and more oblique. The character of the cranial injuries indicates that neither man was wearing a helmet, which is hardly surprising as the evidence generally of grave-goods of this period suggests that helmets, like body armour, were available only to the elite.

The osteological analysis also revealed details of their general health, diet and probable occupation. Both men were about 1.84m (5ft 10ins) in height and were generally well nourished, although the younger man had experienced an episode of iron deficiency anaemia in his youth. The older man suffered from joint degeneration of the spine and shoulders, as well as damage to the vertebral discs in the lower spine, probably the result of carrying heavy loads. Evidence of muscle trauma in his lower limbs may have been due to the same cause and/or to marching long distances. Both men were strongly built and both had upper limb musculature developed as the result of repeated flexion and extension of the forearm, possibly attributable to weapon practice and use. These traits suggest both men had seen military service. In the case of the older man this impression is reinforced by the fact that the front of his skull bore healed compression fractures, such as might have been sustained in some earlier military engagement (*colour plate 14*). Both men still possessed all their teeth at the time of death but, as is common in ancient populations, these exhibited considerable wear owing to the crudity of food-processing techniques. The dental health of the older man, however, left something to be desired as he suffered from plaque concretions, cavities, receding gums and a rather nasty, pus-releasing abscess (*colour plate 15*). Interestingly, in both men the front teeth displayed marked chipping, suggesting these individuals carried out tasks which involved the use of their front teeth as tools. This could, for example, have been the preparation of stringing for bows.

Having established quite clearly that the mass grave was the final resting-place of men involved in the Battle of Chester, there remains the question of whether they were Anglians or Britons. The arrangement of the bodies in the mass grave shows they were interred with some degree of care and order. Furthermore, all the fragments around the injuries were found with the skulls, suggesting burial had taken place soon after death and also that interment had taken place close to the spot where they had fallen. Given that it was Aethelfrith and not the Britons who controlled the area following the battle then it seems very likely that these men represent the heavy losses suffered by Aethelfrith's army. The west-east alignment of the bodies – the usual orientation of Christian burials – would thus be purely fortuitous, as the conversion of Northumbria to Christianity did not begin until the reign of Edwin. Similarly, the absence of weapons in the mass grave (or rather the modest portion of it examined so far) would be explained by the need to recover as many as possible given the vulnerable position of the Northumbrian force.

The notion that these men were English casualties is confirmed by the results of an isotopic analysis of teeth from the two excavated skeletons carried out by Dr Andrew Millard at the Department of Archaeology of Durham University. This technique is based on the fact that people who are born and grow up in a particular geographical region accumulate a combination of stable isotopes in the enamel of their teeth specific to that region; the oxygen and strontium isotopes being especially important in this regard. The possible areas of origin indicated for one of the men are the Peak District and the southern Grampian Mountains. For the other, eastern England either on the coal measures of the Peak District and in a narrow band where the coal measures outcrop extending up to the north-east of England, or the Grampian Mountains or just possibly the Cheviot Hills west of Bamburgh. It is conceivable that these men were from one of the northern British kingdoms who either just happened to be visiting their kin in North Wales at the time of Aethelfrith's attack or were there strengthening alliances. However, the balance of probability favours the theory that these men were Northumbrian warriors in Aethelfrith's army. This view is supported further by new information recovered about the neighbouring fortification.

Turning now to the earthwork fort, the first two seasons of work, in 2002 and 2003, confirmed that its defences had never continued along the river frontage and also that the rampart had indeed been faced with a substantial masonry revetment. Concentrations of heavy rubble had been seen in earlier sections through the ditch fill but a new cut in 2002 found part of the lowest course of the revetment still in place at the front of the rampart (*colour plate 16*). The 2004 investigations showed that, in addition to stones robbed from the ruins of Roman buildings, the revetment included tombstones lifted from the nearby Roman cemeteries lining Watling Street to the north (14 and *colour plates 17 & 18*). The defences exhibited no signs of major repairs or re-castings and this, combined with the complete absence of buildings from the areas of the interior examined so far, suggests it was occupied for a very brief period. If the results obtained from the radiocarbon dating of the skeletons were pleasing, those produced by testing of organic material preserved in the fill of the fort ditch were quite astonishing, at least for the writer, who by the third season of the Heronbridge Project had firmly convinced himself that the earthwork was a Viking Age construction on the basis of its size, form of construction, shape and riverside location. Seeds retrieved from the ditch fill, which was associated with a secondary usage (described below) which had taken place long after the ditch had ceased to function as a defensive obstacle, gave a date range spanning the period from the late seventh to the mid-ninth century. This suggests that the ditch, and thus obviously the fort to which it belonged, was already in existence by *c.*700. In the absence of any other known event in the area comparable with the Battle of Chester it seems highly likely that the fort also was associated with that encounter.

The sources imply that the British either did not have time to construct any sort of defensive position or, following Geoffrey of Monmouth's sources, they simply occupied Chester. In any case, the fort at Heronbridge is clearly positioned as a defence against an attack coming from the south or west, in other words from British territory. On this reasoning, therefore, the fort must have been built by the Northumbrian army, presumably after rather than before its victory. Deep in the heart of hostile country, with his army having just sustained severe losses despite its victory, and knowing the enemy would soon be re-grouping ready to launch a counter-attack Aethelfrith decided against trying to push home his advantage by proceeding further into North Wales. This makes Heronbridge a site of unique importance, as no other Anglo-Saxon fortification built in this period has been found. One other is known, however, from the literary sources and, very interestingly, that lay at Bamburgh – ancestral stronghold of the Bernician royal house. Founded by Ida, Aethelfrith's grandfather, this lay within a hilltop fortification dating back at least to the Bronze Age and is described in the Northern Recension of the *Anglo-Saxon Chronicle* as 'being defended first with a stockade and later a wall' (*sub anno* 547).

Aethelfrith chose a good spot for his camp at Heronbridge (see 7 & 8). The river formed one side, the south rampart was sited along the edge of a steep drop down to the floodplain, while that on the north ran along the edge of a partially silted-up watercourse which had been deepened in the Roman period.[13] The remaining side, the longest, ran parallel with Watling Street and was protected by a substantial ditch. From the top of the rampart there would have been a panoramic view of the surrounding countryside and from a slightly more elevated position, such as the top of a wooden tower or an even simpler construction, it would have been possible to see all the way to the lower slopes of the Halkyn range, nearly ten miles distant to the west. The scale of effort put into the construction of the Heronbridge fortification suggests to the author at least that it was designed not as a temporary base to be abandoned at the end of the campaigning season but as a permanent stronghold to dominate and defend newly won territory in a 'greater Northumbria.' In other words, it was Aethelfrith's intention to project Northumbrian power into the north Midlands and thus, by intimidation if not outright belligerency, prevent a coalition of British, Mercian and East Anglian forces

The existence of surviving organic material in the lower part of the ditch fill was first noted in a section cut in the early 1930s, when lengths of small tree branches were seen. When another section across the ditch was excavated in 2004 further examples were found occurring freely throughout the fill at all levels along with clumps of fibrous material and hundreds of large seeds (*colour plates 17-19*). On analysis, the straw-like fibrous material turned out to be the stems of flax plants with the seeds derived from the same source. Flax was the main material used for linen manufacture and in order to render the flax plant stems into a workable state they had to be soaked or *retted*, as it was termed, in water for a considerable period. It would seem that, long after it had fallen into disuse, the fort ditch took on a second lease of life as a flax-retting tank. Other seeds from the ditch fill belonged to plants and weeds typical of cultivated land and a few indicating that wheat, too, was being grown in the vicinity. Clearly people were working and living permanently in the neighbourhood as early as the beginning or middle of the eighth century. Although impossible to prove at the moment, these people were most likely living at Eccleston, which raises the possibility of continuous occupation in the Heronbridge/Eccleston area for a period of 2,000 years. Indeed, evidence recovered from a section cut through the Roman road a little further south in 1970 suggests that clearance of tree cover in the area had begun well before the Romans arrived, which is what one would expect in an area so attractive for settlement.[14]

IV

FROM CARLEGION TO LEGACAESTIR: MERCIAN CHESTER C.625-C.875

Along with Aethelfrith's throne, Edwin also inherited his territorial ambitions, no doubt much to the disbelief, dismay and downright fury of his erstwhile allies to the south and west. His first move was to annexe the Pennine kingdom of Elmet and drive out its king. Penda, the new ruler in Mercia, appears to have owed allegiance to Edwin and fought against the latter's enemies in Wessex. Despite the shelter and support he had been given there, it was not long before Edwin launched an offensive against Gwynedd, now ruled by his foster-brother Cadwallon. It is hardly surprising that in the Welsh sources he was described as 'Edwin the Deceitful.' There is no mention in the sources of Edwin's aggression being resisted by any ruler in Din Eirth and it may be that the kingdom had not recovered from the losses sustained at the Battle of Chester. By 631 Edwin had driven Cadwallon back first into Anglesey and thence to Ireland. He thus controlled the whole of North Wales. Edwin's conquests marked the greatest extent of Northumbrian domination, but this situation was not to last. Just like the predecessor he had deposed, his adventure in the west came to nothing. Cadwallon returned in 633 and, now supported by Penda of Mercia, took the fight to Edwin. He defeated and killed him at the Battle of Hatfield, near Doncaster, and then spent more than 12 months laying waste to Northumbria. Thus, as some might have said at the time, Edwin got his just desserts for turning on those who had given him sanctuary when he had needed it most. The fact that Edwin took possession of Anglesey, and even the Isle of Man, shows that his forces included a fleet of some size, which almost certainly would have been based at Chester. A poem eulogising Cadwallon, *Moliant Cadwallawn*, does actually refer to the ships of both sides.[1] It is also the first time the term *Cymru* is used to describe the people of Wales.[2]

With depressing inevitability history was to repeat itself several times more during the coming decades. Cadwallon was himself killed in 634 by the new Northumbrian king, Oswald. He quickly re-established control over much of the area taken by Edwin, excluding North Wales, while Penda was allowed to continue in power in Mercia as Oswald's vassal. It was not long before Penda became discontented with this inferior status and he began plotting with his old allies in Wales. In 642 Oswald decided to take steps to deal with this emerging threat and, just like Aethelfrith a quarter of a century earlier, he set out with an army to make the long journey to North Wales. The clash happened at *Cocboy* or *Maserfeld* near Oswestry, where Oswald was defeated and killed. Being a prominent Christian, Oswald was accorded martyr status and his cult became firmly established in the area. Indeed, Oswestry – the name means 'St. Oswald's tree' – was supposedly named after him and the field where the Roman Catholic church now stands is believed to be the site of the battle.

Penda's victory at Maserfeld led to a second ravaging of Northumbria, this time as far north as Bamburgh. In an attempt to break the pattern of alternating victory and defeat a settlement was reached in which the two constituent kingdoms of Northumbria were re-established, Oswine ruling in Deira and Oswiu in Bernicia, with both marrying members of Penda's family. The Mercian king's actions, however, were not motivated solely by a wish to see an end to the bloodshed; he had other ambitions which relied on peace in the North. In 645 Penda defeated Cenwealh of Wessex and in 654, with the support of his Welsh allies, he attacked and killed King Anna of East Anglia. Thus, within the space of little more than a decade, Penda had become virtual ruler of the whole of England. However, it was very far from being a single and unified nation. Three years earlier, Oswiu had contrived the murder of Oswine of Deira. Occupied with other matters, Penda had installed a client ruler, Aethelwald, in Deira to forestall Oswiu's attempt to reunite Northumbria. By 655, Penda decided that Oswiu had to be removed and campaigned against him as far north as the Forth, accompanied by Aethelwald along with Aethelhere and Cadafael, the client rulers he had installed in East Anglia and Gwynedd respectively. They laid siege to Oswiu but departed when he handed over a large tribute he had collected. On the return journey south Aethelwald and Cadafael deserted Penda, who was left to face the pursuing Oswiu alone. In a battle fought near Leeds Penda was killed. For the next three years, Oswiu ruled in Mercia and also campaigned in Wales. Peada, Penda's heir, was allowed to rule in Mercia south of the Trent until he was killed at the instigation of his wife, Oswiu's daughter. In 659 the ealdormen of Mercia rebelled, led by Wulfhere, another of Penda's sons, and regained their independence. Warfare continued intermittently until 675 when Archbishop Theodore, Penda's youngest son, negotiated a peace between

Ethelred, Wulfhere's successor, and Ecgfrith of Northumbria that was to last into the eighth century.

During the turbulent third quarter of the seventh century Din Eirth, later Powys, regained something of its former political and military power. Early bardic fragments refer to its ruler Cynddylan, son of Cyndrwyn, another of the Cadelling line, commemorated in the elegy *Marwnnd Cynddylan* ('The Lament for Cynddylan').[3] Present at the battle of Old Oswestry in 642, he is recorded as later attacking Gwynedd – presumably against Cadafael following Penda's death – and also beyond the *Tren* (the River Tern in Shropshire) and into western Mercia as far as *Caer Lwytgoed* – probably Lichfield. Inevitably, this resulted in reprisal raids following Wulfhere's accession. These culminated in the defeat and death in battle of Cynddylan and his brothers, followed by the destruction of his stronghold at *Pengwern* ('Hall of the Welsh'). These events are also described in a prose and verse saga known as *Canu Heledd* ('The Song of Heledd'), one of a series of dramatic monologues by Cynddylan's sister Heledd as she gazes down on *Pengwern* from a neighbouring hill at the blazing ruins of her home. These poems survive as part of a ninth-century saga known as the *Canu Llywarch Hen* and it is clear that memories of these earlier events were being deployed to reinforce the sense of loss inspired by the conquest of Powys by Mercia in the 820s.[4] The death of Cynddylan and the destruction of Pengwern must have been equally traumatic to be remembered for so long:

> Cynddylan the bright buttress of the borderland, wearing a chain,
> stubborn in battle, he defended Tren, his father's town.
> How sad it is to lay the white flesh in the black coffin,
> Cynddylan the leader of a hundred hosts.
> The hall of Cynddylan is still tonight, after losing its chief;
> great merciful God, what shall I do?
> The eagle of Pengwern, grey-crested, uplifted is his cry,
> greedy for the flesh of Cynddylan.
> The chapels of Bassa are his resting place tonight, his last welcome,
> the pillar of battle, the heart of the men of Argoed ...
> The white town in the valley, glad is the kite at the bloodshed of battle;
> its people have perished ...
> I have looked out on a lovely land from the mound of Gorwynnion;
> long is the sun's course – longer are my memories ...
>
> (*Canu Heledd*)

Despite the lateness of the versions which have survived, the poems about Cynddylan are useful for the information they contain about the extent of his kingdom. From the mention of places and features such as *Bassa* (Baschurch) and *Ercall* (now represented by Childs Ercall and High Ercall), the Rivers Severn and Tern and the Wrekin it is clear that this included much of west Shropshire and south-east Montgomeryshire. Various attempts have been made to identify the site of *Pengwern*. The most likely is the Berth by Baschurch. This is a defended glacial hillock protected by a rampart and inturned entrance, linked by causeways across an area of marsh, and close to the spot where Cynddylan is supposed to have been buried. Wroxeter appears to have been abandoned as a population centre by the middle of the seventh century, yet Shrewsbury was not founded until the early eighth century on present evidence. *Pengwern* may thus have been the intermediate centre, a relocation caused by the inceasingly hostile relations between Mercia and its British neighbours as the seventh century wore on.

By the end of the seventh century, the territory of the *Wreocensaetna*, including Cheshire, was fully under Anglian control. Mercia had consolidated its control over the kingdoms surrounding it, gradually absorbing them into a Greater Mercia. Bede, writing around AD 740, gives the Anglicised names for both Chester (*Legacaestir*) and Bangor-is-y-Coed (*Bancornaburg*) and makes the point that these are the current forms. After a period of relative peace during the latter part of the seventh century the first half of the eighth century saw a return to warfare. This time the combatants were not Mercia versus Northumbria – the latter had dissolved into civil war, never to regain its former pre-eminence – but variously Mercia versus Wessex, Mercia versus the Welsh kingdoms, and on occasion both of these English kingdoms against the Welsh. Much of the initial Anglo-British conflict appears to have been along the southern border of Wales, judging from what the sources tell us, and they also reveal that little territorial gain was made by either side. It is to this period that the earliest of the surviving frontier-delineating earthworks belong. In the northern Marches this means Wat's Dyke, which runs from Basingwerk on the shore of the Dee estuary, west and south of Northop, then east of Mold and continuing along the east bank of the River Alyn through Hope via Wrexham to the south. Even today the place-names of this area remain predominantly English, despite subsequent re-absorption into Wales. Basingwerk is an example of the *inge*-type place-name considered to denote particularly early English settlement. There are also examples of the 'forest clearance'-type, representing the bringing of new areas under cultivation: places such as Bagillt Bacca's *leah*, Penley Penda's *leah*, Buckley, Honkley and so on.

The renewed Mercian expansion westwards during the first half of the eighth century, rather than demoralising the neighbouring Welsh, appears to have had the opposite effect, and we find a resurgent Din Eirth – now Powys – under its ruler Eliseg. The latter is commemorated on a monument known as 'Eliseg's Pillar' near Llangollen, erected by his great-grandson Cyngen, who ruled Powys a century later. The Mercian aggression was led by Aethelbald, who came to the throne in 716 following the death of Ceolred, the last of Penda's line, during a drunken fit. Aethelbald ruled for over four decades but in 752 Mercia suffered a major defeat by the forces of Wessex at the Battle of Burford and this led to a period of unrest, which culminated five years later in Aethelbald's assassination by a member of his own bodyguard. After nearly twelve months of uncertainty a clear successor emerged in the person of Offa, whose reign – at 39 years – not only very nearly equalled Aethelbald's in terms of duration but easily surpassed it in the success and prestige it brought to Mercia. Offa achieved supremacy over all the English kingdoms south of the Humber and was regarded by continental rulers such as Charlemagne and Pope Hadrian as *Rex Anglorum*, 'King of the English,' something which none of his predecessors had attained. The Welsh tested the strength of the new ruler early in his reign by increasing their raids into Mercia. However, a Welsh force of some considerable size was caught near Hereford in 760 and defeated. There was a marked decline in raids thereafter and this allowed Offa to concentrate on subduing his English neighbours. It was some years before his attention again turned to Wales, but in 777 he staged a major invasion of the kingdom of Deheubarth in the south. In 783 the *Welsh Annals* record that he mounted another campaign. This was on a far grander scale than any previous incursion and is described in the *Annals* as the 'devastation of Britain'. He was obviously trying to achieve a serious weakening of Welsh military power, most probably to ease the way for the construction of the great frontier earthwork that bears his name, Offa's Dyke. Although extensive investigation has failed to provide firm dating evidence for its construction there seems no reason to doubt the claim in Asser's *Life of King Alfred* that Offa 'built a great dyke between England and Wales'.[5]

The entry in the *Anglo-Saxon Chronicle* actually says that this ran 'from sea to sea', a phrase which caused many researchers to try and discover the 'lost' section of the dyke running between Treuddyn and the coast somewhere near Prestatyn. As a consequence of more than 30 years' fieldwork led by David Hill, it can now be seen that this search was in vain, for this supposed final section never existed.[6] Instead, it seems that the earlier Wat's Dyke, which runs parallel with and about 5km east of Offa's Dyke northwards from the confluence of the Rivers Vyrnwy and Morda to the Dee estuary at Basingwerk, continued to mark the frontier in this sector.

In 786, rivalry between competing branches of the ruling family in Wessex culminated in a situation which enabled Offa to place his own candidate, Beorhtric, on the throne, and the following year the new king married one of Offa's daughters. Another daughter was married to Aelflaed, King of Northumbria, in 792, further extending Offa's control over the other English kingdoms. Then, in 794, he took action of a more direct kind when he invaded East Anglia and killed its ruler King Aethelberht. *De facto* ruler of all England and at the height of his powers, Offa died on 29 July 796. His son and successor Ecgfrith died 141 days later and without heirs. This premature end of the dynasty signalled the beginning of a slow decline in Mercia's fortunes. The fact that Cenwulf, Ecgfrith's successor, campaigned in north-east Wales very soon after his accession implies that Powys was testing the strength of the new king. Cenwulf won a battle at Rhuddlan in 797 and the following year he launched an attack against Gwynedd, killing its king Caradog in an encounter near Offa's Dyke. This settled matters on the Welsh border for some years. The opening years of the ninth century saw Cenwulf successfully resisting a Northumbrian invasion but losing suzerainty over Wessex. In 816 he invaded the provinces of Rhufoniog and Eryri close to Snowdonia and two years later he was campaigning in Dyfed at the other end of Wales. He died at Basingwerk, near Flint, in 821, where he was presumably engaged in mounting a further attack on Gwynedd. Ceolwulf, his successor, continued this work, destroying the ancient stronghold of Gwynedd at Deganwy in 822 and taking direct control of Powys. But soon afterwards the internal rivalries in Mercia came to a head and Ceolwulf was banished. One outcome was that the rulers of Powys regained control of their kingdom so once more Chester was on the frontier. Mercia was humbled in 829 when Egbert of Wessex invaded and took over the whole kingdom. The peaceful submission of the Northumbrians followed as Egbert's army rested near Sheffield. The following year saw the Welsh kingdoms also agreeing terms with the new 'overlord.' That same year saw Wiglaf managing to restore Mercian independence. But it had lost the primacy which Penda had once wrested from Northumbria. This now passed to Wessex, just as new players in the game of power the Vikings arrived on the scene.

ARCHAEOLOGY

As far as Chester is concerned, the period which saw the ascendancy of Mercia is an almost total blank in both the literary and the archaeological record. We have no means of knowing, for example, if the clash with Aethelfrith had unfortunate repercussions for the site and, if so, how severe they were. The complete absence of pagan Anglo-Saxon burials from Cheshire suggests the bulk of Anglian settlement occurred after the conversion of the English kingdoms in the second quarter of the seventh century. Excepting the isolated example at Wroxeter mentioned in the previous chapter, there is the parallel lack of memorial stones that occur so frequently in what was to become Wales. Thus, along the Welsh Marches there is a broad zone where archaeological evidence indicative of culture or race is non-existent.

The establishment of a definitive frontier in the form of Wat's Dyke some 15km to the west of Chester would have created a more secure environment for the settlement's development during the second half of the seventh century. The church of St John, located beside the ruins of the amphitheatre just outside the south-east angle of the fortress defences, is reputed to have been founded in 689.[7] Certainly this would fit with the conversion of Mercia after Penda's death, when many new churches and monasteries were founded throughout the kingdom. The choice of location is interesting. The ruined amphitheatre would certainly have afforded a ready supply of building stone. It may also have already possessed a religious significance if it was the scene of Christian martyrdoms during the occasional persecutions of the later Roman Empire (amphitheatres were the specified venue for public executions). In this case St John's may have been a re-dedication and/or rebuilding of a pre-existing church or shrine. As suggested above, another possible reason for the siting of St John's here rather than inside the fortress was because the latter was already under the control of another church. In their description of the transfer of the relics of St Werburgh to Chester in 875 the medieval chroniclers relate how they were placed in an existing church *of reputedly high antiquity* dedicated to SS Peter & Paul which was subsequently rebuilt and re-dedicated to the Mercian saint when the Lady Aethelflaed restored Chester in 907.[8] The location of this church is known because St Werburgh's later became an abbey and then the cathedral. That at least one church existed in Chester by the early ninth century is indicated by two pieces of sculpture, both now in the British Museum. One is a fragment of an elaborately entangled animal carving; the other is a modest headstone with simple interlacings and an attractive animal portrait (see *17*). The two principal members of the famous group of crosses at Sandbach, with their interlace patternwork and scenes from the New Testament, illustrate the richness and complexity of sculpture in this period. The only inscribed memorial of this period from the whole of the county was found in a church at Upton just outside Chester. Re-used as building material it had originally stood in Overchurch on the Wirral. One face of the stone carries a decorative scheme in the form of a pair of interlaced dragons, a design paralleled on coins of Offa from the end of the eighth century. The inscription, in Anglian runes, reads:

The community erected this monument …

Pray for Aethelmund ['s soul]

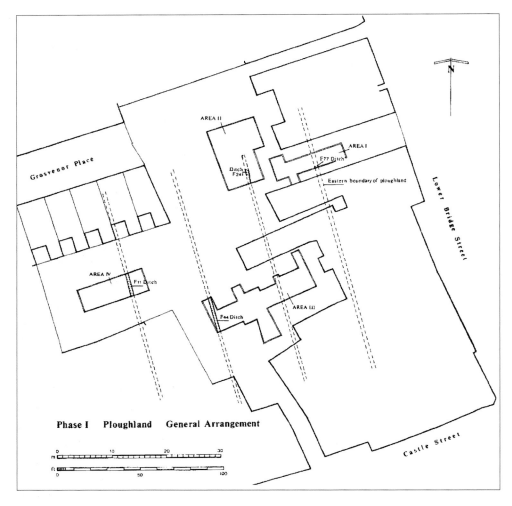

15 Lower Bridge Street (west) excavation 1974-6. Plan of plough-strips. © *Chester City Council*

While Chester was probably an ecclesiastical centre in this period – as earlier – did it amount to anything more than this? The mass production of coinage for the first time since the Roman period during the reign of Offa indicates a return to a monetary-based economy. It also means that where they are in circulation in large numbers coins again become a useful indicator of the degree of activity and intensity of occupation. However, apart from one site shortly to be mentioned, they are completely absent from the north-west Midlands. Higham interprets the lack of such *sceatta* coins from Chester to mean that it was not yet a 'port of any consequence'.[9] Yet he also views the absence of coinage from the region as a whole to indicate that 'what local trading occurred was almost certainly conducted by barter'.[10] Clearly, therefore, the absence of coinage of this period does not necessarily mean a lack of either substantial populations or significant commercial activity. Chester was important as a sea-port in the Roman period – indeed, that is why it was founded at this spot – and it functioned as such again in the tenth century. Not just for mercantile trade either, because in both those periods it was also an important naval base. As mentioned above, it may well have been the base for Edwin's fleet in the 630s. There seems every likelihood, to the writer at least, that Chester was the focus of a certain amount of seaborne trade in the eighth and ninth centuries, both up and down the west coast and across the Irish Sea. That this has left little trace in the archaeological record is not surprising if, just as in both the preceding and later periods, the goods being imported were overwhelmingly of a perishable nature. Slaves and hunting-dogs were prominent exports from Britain at the time of its invasion by Rome and the former were certainly an important commodity again from the fifth century onwards – witness the story of St Patrick. Similarly, the regulations governing the port at Chester in the eleventh century refer to marten pelts as the chief import from Ireland.

That such seaborne trade was carried on, if only intermittently, cannot be doubted. The site at Meols mentioned previously has produced two Frisian *sceattas* of the eighth century, three Northumbrian *styca* coins of the ninth century and a Frankish-style strap terminal, and it seems that occupation of this coastal trading settlement continued unbroken throughout this period. Griffiths is of the opinion that the finds point to imports 'arriving sporadically, reflecting a mixture of settlement and the occasional use of Meols as a "beach market"'.[11] Ships would have visited the site during the summer sailing season and there may well have been regular fairs held at certain festivals during the year. As Griffiths also notes, stuck out on the end of the Wirral peninsula and easily accessible by sea from Wales, Ireland, the Isle of Man and Northumbria, Meols was ideally positioned as a the equivalent of a modern freeport, unencumbered by royal dues and tax officials. It may also have been the point where pilgrims landed on their way to a shrine located on nearby Hilbre Island.

Although our understanding of the character and extent of occupation in Chester during the period covered by this chapter is still in its infancy, excavations over the last thirty years have provided the first pieces of tangible evidence. Along those parts of its circuit unaffected by either medieval demolition or Civil War damage, long stretches of the fortress wall still survive largely intact to the present day and it is reasonable to assume that the rest of the legionary defences were still largely upstanding in the period under discussion. However, as described in chapter two, a long section south of the east gate had almost certainly collapsed by 800. Because of their massiveness and robust construction the gate-structures would have continued into the Mercian era. Much of the superstructure of the Roman east gate, up to and including the arches of its double portals, was found incorporated within its medieval successor when the latter was demolished in 1768, and there is no reason to suppose that the other gates did not survive to the same extent.[12] The interval towers, however, were probably largely ruinous.

The barracks and many of the other lesser buildings appear, from the evidence of excavations in various parts of the fortress, to have long since decayed to the point where they were no more than low mounds of rubble. On a number of sites within the fortress evidence for cultivation has been found. At Abbey Green, for example, situated next to the city wall east of the Northgate, a layer of soil over 400mm thick was found overlying the fortress intervallum road and the tail of the rampart.[13] Sealed by another road laid down in the tenth century, this soil was well mixed, with no evidence of layers within it, and contained a broad range of artefacts ranging in date from the Roman period to the tenth century. Had this been an entirely natural accumulation some form of stratification would be expected and its formation has instead been attributed to cultivation, possibly involving ploughing. This interpretation is supported by the discovery nearby of a substantial corn-drying oven. This was built a little way to the south, over the remains of one of the centurion's houses. Excavation in 1972–3 of the Northgate Brewery site, occupying an equivalent position west of the Northgate, revealed a similar deposit. This was slighter, however, and there was no major damage to the underlying Roman stratigraphy, so the plough does not appear to have been employed. Either this area was used for horticulture or manual tilling was involved.[14] A similar picture was found around the same time on a site excavated at Goss Street, in the central part of the fortress immediately west of the headquarters building.[15] A soil accumulation of a rather different nature was revealed a few years later at the Hunter Street School excavation, located approximately mid-way between the last two sites mentioned. Here, across the area of an open compound belonging to a late Roman building, the deposit in question was much darker in colour and with a richer organic appearance. These characteristics make it much closer in form to the 'dark earth' deposit recognised in a number of English towns and cities which formed during the interval between the Roman and Anglo-Saxon periods.[16] A variety of explanations have been put forward to account for these deposits, but it is unlikely that 'one theory explains all'. It is more probable that different processes occurred in different places. In the case of the Hunter Street School site, it has been proposed that the 'dark earth' formed as the result of using the open space left by the compound of the Roman building for the herding and penning of cattle.[17] In all of the above cases, dating of the agricultural activity was impossible because of the absence of contemporary artefacts. However, given that it took place over a considerable period and continued into the time when pottery once more became commonly available – around the middle of the tenth century – this activity most probably began in the ninth or possibly even the eighth century.

Clearly, in Mercian Chester, there were extensive open areas within the old fortress where low mounds of uneven ground covered by vegetation marked the former sites of the less substantial Roman buildings. Interspersed with these were patches of land under cultivation together with corrals or pens for animals and barns or lesser stores for produce. Presumably, there would also have been dwellings almost certainly built of timber scattered about, unless the land was worked entirely by a monastic community centred on SS Peter & Paul. In contrast, there would have been some parts of the fortress where the more substantial fortress buildings still stood largely intact or at least as very impressive ruins. With walls over a metre thick, much of the baths complex was presumably still upstanding and most of its concrete roof-vaults were probably still intact. Possibly by now, however, the roof of the exercise-hall had begun to deteriorate and may even have collapsed altogether. The same may have been true of the cross-hall in the *principia*. Elsewhere, the Elliptical Building was probably just a shell by now, even if its very substantial walls still stood metres high. Because of its robust construction and modest size, the neighbouring bath-building was very likely still largely intact. Indeed, when excavated in 1968-9, the walls of the latter were found surviving to a height of a metre or more above Roman ground level, and in several rooms the hypocaust system was still completely intact.[18]

Beyond the fortress defences the picture would have been equally varied. Assuming that St John's church was founded in the late seventh century then its construction would have initiated the process of the dismantling of the amphitheatre for building stone which, by the middle of the tenth century, had reduced significant sections of its outer wall on the south side to ground level. A church at this spot may also have become a focus for secular occupation in the Mercian period, especially in view of its close proximity to the river and the potential for mercantile trade. Excavations west of Lower Bridge Street in the mid-1970s revealed evidence of pre-tenth-century ploughing.[19] The area had been cultivated by dividing it up into north–south strips approximately 12m wide separated by small drainage ditches (*15*). The ploughsoil was formed out of churned-up Roman refuse deposits and natural soil which survived intact in the 15-20m wide undisturbed zone left between the edge of the cultivation area and the Roman road which ran down to the – presumably still functioning – bridge over the Dee. Numerous striation marks made by the plough-tip were found in the surface of the underlying natural clay. The cultivated area continued westwards for at least 50m and four 'plough-strips' were found within the area examined. The date when this activity began is unknown but it evidently continued for many, many decades. Eventually, the ploughing ceased and the drainage/boundary ditches separating the plough-strips were left to silt up. Possibly a change of ownership resulted in a change of use. Alternatively, the crop yield may have declined owing to exhaustion of the relatively poor soil.

After an interval of unknown duration, the peace of the Lower Bridge site was temporarily interrupted by a brief spate of activity, which saw the excavation and use of at least three 'roasting-pits,' along with the construction of a small kiln or oven. The context and meaning of this activity are unknown. It could represent the remains of a giant 'barbecue' associated with the celebration of a festival. Then again, it could indicate the temporary encampment of a body of soldiers, such as the brief stay by the Viking army in 893. The next event on the site, probably following on shortly afterwards, was the construction of a small, sunken-featured building; to be more accurate this was little more than a hut (16). Only its eastern end survived but this was sufficient to show it measured about 3m north–south by a minimum of 2.5m east–west.[20] The floor of the sunken area lay 0.40m below external ground level and cut into this in a central position at the east end was a trio of shallow post-settings. A single external post-setting was found a short distance back from the edge of the sunken area. This lay at the mid-point of the east end of the structure, which suggests it supported one end of a ridge-pole. If so, the hut would have had sides which sloped down steeply to the ground. The sunken area may have been floored over with planks, in which case the three posts in the bottom may have supported a part of the floor which bore a heavy weight such as a clay and stone hearth. Alternatively, the base of the sunken area could have been the floor.

No artefacts were recovered to date this modest structure and so it can merely be suggested, on the grounds of its position in the overall chronological sequence of the site, that it belongs in the period c.850–c.900. Ironically, a small collection of objects of this very period was found nearby – sadly mixed in with the fill of a much later feature which had destroyed their original context – but their quality shows quite clearly that they belonged to someone far higher up the social scale than the occupants of the hut. The items in question consist of two sherds of pottery and a silver brooch. The pottery belongs to a type classified as 'Red-Burnished Wares' and they are the only known examples from the whole of Chester. This type of pottery is dated to the eighth and ninth centuries and is thought to be northern French in origin.[21] It is quite rare on the Continent and even rarer in Britain where, apart from the Chester example, vessels are known only at Ipswich and Hamwih, near Southampton. The last-named sites were two of the principal maritime trading centres – known as *wics* or *emporia* – in the country. The brooch – described in greater detail in

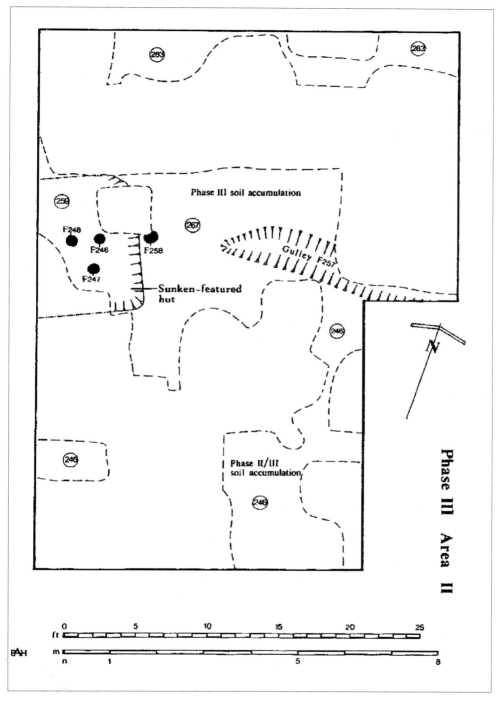

16 Lower Bridge Street (west) excavation 1974. Plan of remains of ninth-century sunken-featured hut and adjacent gulley. © *Chester City Council*

17 Ninth-century grave-slab found somewhere in Chester. © *British Museum*

chapter six – is a small disc-shaped example of openwork form decorated with an elaborate interlace design and incorporating tiny pieces of blue glass (*colour plate 20*). While there is a chance that these objects were associated with the next phase of activity on the Lower Bridge Site, that which followed the founding of the *burh* in 907, it is equally, if not more, likely that they belonged to someone living hereabouts during the ninth century. If so, then it is very interesting that a person possessing the wealth to afford such luxuries was residing in this part of the city at this time.

Only one Roman building is known in the near vicinity of the Lower Bridge site and that was the large courtyard building tentatively interpreted as a *mansio* or official lodgings which stood on the edge of the escarpment looking out across the Dee. Much of this was demolished in the mid-fourth century and so the building is unlikely to have been a significant feature of the landscape by this period.[22] Substantial Roman buildings occupied the land between the west defences of the fortress and the harbour area, but where these have been examined it was found that their ruins were ransacked for reusable stone when the establishments of several religious orders were built here in the twelfth century.[23] Consequently, any evidence relating to the intervening period had been destroyed. One Roman building which definitely would have been a prominent landmark in this part of Mercian Chester, because of its robust masonry and concrete structures, was the enormous bathing complex which occupied the area now defined by Lower Watergate Street, the city walls, Stanley Place and Stanley Street.[24] One other feature in this general area to be mentioned, if only in passing, is the wall of massive masonry which runs along the foot of the river-cliff, at the edge of what is now the Roodee racecourse, below and roughly parallel with the city wall. Variously interpreted as either a Roman quay wall or a defensive wall of the later Roman period, this is discussed in more detail in chapter six.

Evidence for activity in the immediate hinterland of Chester in this period has recently come to light. It was described in the previous chapter how the place-name Eccleston suggests the existence of a settled Christian community encountered by the first Anglian colonists moving into the area; in other words that there were people living at Eccleston by the mid-seventh century. The community here could have originated in the sub-Roman period, possibly founded by the inhabitants of Heronbridge who, for some reason, had found that site no longer suitable. Indirect evidence for the existence of a settlement at Eccleston by the eighth century has now been provided by the recent excavations at Heronbridge.[25] The sectioning of the ditch of the earthwork fort at a point mid-way along the side running parallel with Eaton Road revealed the fill to be rich in well-preserved organic material, namely clumps of fibrous material and large seeds. Beneath this, in the bottom of the ditch, there was a layer of large blocks of stone derived from the revetment at the front of the adjacent rampart. The stones formed a reasonably level and consistent layer suggesting they had been placed there deliberately rather than having merely tumbled into the ditch when the front of the rampart eventually collapsed (*colour plates 17 & 18*). This impression was confirmed when subsequent analysis of the organic material revealed that it consisted largely of the stems and seeds of flax plants (*colour plate 19*). Flax plants were used to make linen and one of the early stages of the process required the stems to be soaked in water for long periods in order to make them malleable. This was a process known as 'retting'. Clearly, therefore, at some time after the demise of the fort, one or more lengths of its ditch had been transformed into a flax-retting trough. Two flax seeds retrieved from the fill were selected for radiocarbon dating. The results were AD 650–830 cal (95% confidence) and AD 680–775 cal (68% confidence) and AD 710–980 cal (95%

confidence) and AD 770–890 cal (68% confidence) respectively.[26] Other seeds from the ditch fill belonged to plants and weeds typical of cultivated land and a few indicating that wheat, too, was being grown in the vicinity. This evidence indicates that people were cultivating the land and living permanently in the neighbourhood by c.750. This reinforces the impression that there was continuity of occupation in the Heronbridge/Eccleston area from late Roman times right through to the early Middle Ages.

V

DESCENT OF THE VIKINGS
AND CHESTER REFORTIFIED

The first Viking raid on the British coast occurred at the end of the eighth century when, on 8 June 793, they assaulted the great Northumbrian monastery at Lindisfarne. This event caused shockwaves of horror across Western Europe. Piratical acts by some of the Northmen were not unknown. A charter of Offa issued in the previous year speaks of the need to defend Kent from these pirates and in 807 King Cenwulf paid them a ransom to release a priest who had fallen into their clutches. But the raid of 793 was of a different order; its destructiveness, savagery and boldness were completely unexpected. Monasteries on Raithlin Island, County Antrim, and Iona were attacked in 795. The mid-ninth century saw Viking raiders overwintering in Ireland, including the establishment of a naval encampment or *longphort* at Dublin in 841. The *Anglo-Saxon Chronicle* records a major raid on Lindsey in 838 and another in 842 in which there was great slaughter at both London and Rochester. London was again the target nine years later. King Beorhtwulf of Mercia and his army, or *fyrd*, were put to flight, but when the Danes pressed on into West Saxon territory they were defeated and sustained losses greater than any previously experienced.[1] This demonstrated to the rulers of the English kingdoms that they needed to co-operate if they were to stand any chance of defeating this new and common enemy. Perhaps because the Welsh had sought to take advantage of the situation, or possibly to test the practicalities of deployment in the field, or both, the forces of Wessex and Mercia undertook a joint campaign in Wales in 852. This was very successful and early the following year the alliance was strengthened when King Aethelwulf of Wessex gave his daughter, Aethelswith, in marriage to King Burgred of Mercia.

The Viking threat first came close to our own area in the 850s. As recorded in the Welsh and Irish annals, a raiding party led by a man named Orm laid waste to Anglesey and by 855 was active in the Wrekin area of Shropshire. They were eventually defeated by the Welsh themselves, led by Rhodri Mawr. Ten years later, in 865, the nature of the Danish attacks changed from one of raiding, and even overwintering, to one of conquest and permanent settlement. That year saw the arrival of the *micel here* or 'great raiding army.' This was a formidable force not merely because of its size (it was transported by a fleet exceeding the 350 ships employed in the raid on London in 851), but also because it was led by men who used to great effect the information about the political and military strengths of the English kingdoms gleaned from previous raids. They made landfall in East Anglia, whose rulers submitted very quickly and were compelled to provide quarters for the army through the winter. The following spring, equipped with plenty of horses by the East Angles and having identified the easiest target, the Great Army moved through Mercia and then attacked and captured York. The Northumbrians counter-attacked the following year and managed to breach the walls, but were then caught up in vicious street-fighting in which their losses were so great that they were forced to retreat. The kingdom was now in Viking hands.

In 868 the Danes descended on Mercia and established themselves in a fortress at Nottingham. This was besieged by a combined West Saxon and Mercian force, but no conclusive engagement occurred and some form of agreement was reached between Burgred and the Danes. The latter returned to East Anglia in 870 and successfully put down a rebellion by King Edmund, who was killed. Campaigns against the West Saxons followed and in 871 the Vikings occupied London once more. To buy them off, 'an immense tribute' was collected and handed over to them; the first instance of Danegeld.[2] Following the quelling of a revolt in Northumbria in 873 the Vikings advanced into Mercia the following year, capturing Repton with its mausoleum of the Mercian royal family. Mercia was forced to submit and Burgred was driven into exile. He embarked on a pilgrimage to Rome, where he died soon afterwards. His wife, Aethelswith, lived on in Rome for another 14 years, eventually dying in Pavia, where she was buried.

As well as the capture of Repton the year 875 also saw the reappearance of Chester in the historical record after a gap of nearly three hundred years. According to both the fourteenth-century Chester monk Ranulph Higden and the *Annales Cestrienses* it was at this time that the remains of St Werburgh were transferred from Hanbury (Staffordshire) to a college of secular canons in Chester for safekeeping. The *Annales* describe the event thus:

> In the same year, when the Danes made their winter quarters at Repton after the flight of Burgred, king of the Mercians, the men of Hanbury fearing for themselves, fled to Chester as to a place which was very safe from the butchery of the barbarians, taking with them in a litter the body of St Werburgh, which then for the first time was resolved into dust.
>
> Christie (ed.) 1886, 13

Having secured control of Mercia, the Danes split their forces. One part, under Halfdan, ravaged Northumbria and raided into the lands of the Strathclyde British and the Picts. The other, led by Guthrun, returned to East Anglia and then attacked Wessex. This second group got as far as the Exeter area, but was eventually forced to make terms and surrender hostages by Alfred, who had succeeded to the throne of Wessex in 871. In 877 they retreated northwards, beginning their settlement of Northumbria in earnest and leaving Ceolwulf in charge of western Mercia. Some of the Viking force, a fleet of 23 ships according to Asser, overwintered in Dyfed and in 878 they set out for Wessex, partnered by a land force from further north to trap Alfred in a pincer movement. He was forced to seek refuge in the Somerset marshes – the famous 'burning of the cakes' episode – where he built fortifications on the Isle of Athelney. Alfred eventually regrouped his forces and pushed the Danes out of Wessex the following year.

In Wales, Rhodri Mawr and his son Gwriad were killed in a battle with the English in 878. It may be that the Welsh were seeking to take advantage of the recently weakened Mercia and miscalculated. Ceolwulf II did not outlive the Welsh ruler by very long for he died at some time before 883, possibly at the Battle of Conwy in 881, which the *Annales Cambriae* describe as 'vengeance for Rhodri at God's hand'. Of the surviving *ealdormen*, or earls, a certain Aethelred, whose lands lay in the southern Mercia, achieved a position of pre-eminence, working with and supporting his fellow *ealdormen* and eventually becoming king in all but name. He also established an alliance with Alfred of Wessex, one that was to enable both their kingdoms to regain their losses and roll back Viking power. In 886 Alfred led an army into the lower Thames valley, occupied London and then handed it over to Aethelred, in whose former territory it lay. This gave the English the potential to deny Viking fleets access to both Wessex and Mercia. Although equals in many ways, Aethelred deferred to Alfred's clear superiority in terms of power and authority.[3] Alfred was the senior partner but there are various strands of evidence to show that Aethelred exercised complete authority within his own territory and was not simply Alfred's vassal. Theirs was a mutual agreement, one that involved respect for the other's authority but also recognised the political and military realities. On his coinage Alfred styled himself 'King of the Angles and the Saxons', indicating the equality of the two peoples. However, the fact that Aethelred did not issue any coinage in his own name reflects the truth of the situation. Their alliance, as usual in the times, was reinforced by marriage. Aethelred married Alfred's eldest daughter Aethelflaed. The fact that the daughters of Alfred's family were married to other independent rulers rather than ealdormen is a further indication of Aethelred's special status.

Cheshire, along with the rest of north-west Mercia, seems to have escaped this turbulent period relatively unscathed. To help him in his work to revive learning in Wessex, Alfred summoned a number of scholars and priests, most of whom came from western Mercia. They included Werfrith from Worcester as well as Plegmund, who is traditionally associated with Cheshire.[4] This period of comparative calm came to an abrupt end in 893. The previous year, two Danish armies arrived in Kent. One, a force with 250 ships, built itself a fort at Appledore; the other, led by Hastein with 80 ships, constructed a base at Benfleet. Alfred tried to keep them subdued by a mix of negotiation and shows of force, but their raids intensified and they were frequently joined by Danish armies from East Anglia and Northumbria. Led by Alfred's son Edward, the West Saxons defeated the Appledore Danes at Farnham in 893 and then, joined by Aethelred with a Mercian army, laid siege to the survivors who had sought refuge on the island of Thorney in the River Colne in Hertfordshire. Edward soon had to withdraw, as the annual term of service by his men was coming to an end, but Aethelred persisted with the siege. The possibility of assistance from Alfred was negated by an attack by a Danish fleet on both the north and the south coasts of Devon. The Danes were forced to sue for peace and were allowed to leave after surrendering hostages. Yet Hastein set out on another raid soon after this. Reinforcements from Wessex reached London, allowing Edward and Aethelred to march on the Viking base at Benfleet in Hastein's absence. They broke through the defences, slaughtered the Viking defenders and captured their booty, ships and families. They broke up or burnt most of the Viking fleet, towing the remainder to London or Rochester. On his return, Hastein built a new base at Shoeburyness, followed by another on Mersea Island. Reinforced by Danes from other parts of Britain, they subsequently launched three spectacular raids into western Mercia, one of which focused on Chester.

The first raid, early in 893, advanced up the Thames valley until it came to the borders of the Welsh (*Britannorum*), and then turned north to follow the Severn valley. The Danes were shadowed by a combined force of West Saxons, Mercians and Welsh, who eventually caught up with them at Buttington, near Welshpool. Here they were besieged for many weeks until, running very short of food, they made a dash for their base in Essex. This they achieved, but not without suffering a severe mauling by the Anglo-Welsh force. The Danes then regrouped and gathered further forces, made safe their wives, ships and goods in East Anglia, and embarked upon a second raid late in the same year. Marching day and night and foregoing opportunities for extensive pillaging they reached Chester before the Mercian army could intercept them. The *Anglo-Saxon Chronicle* says that the Danes 'came to a deserted [or a waste] Roman site in the Wirral, called Chester' ('*anre westre ceastre on Wirhealum, seo is Legaceaster gehaten*'). This statement gave rise to the belief that the city was completely unpopulated and it was once thought that Chester was abandoned at some time in the fifth century and remained so until its refortification in the opening years of the tenth century. We saw in previous chapters, however, that there is a growing, if still modest, body of archaeological evidence to show that was not the case. Also, it was apparently thought a place of reasonable security when St Werburgh's remains were transferred here two decades earlier. Another suggestion was that it had only become desolate a short time before 893.[5] While this is possible there is evidence, admittedly little more than circumstantial, which contradicts this picture. For example, Roger of Wendover's version of the *Anglo-Saxon Chronicle* states that the Danish army gained entry to the city with the aid of Scandinavians among the resident population who acted as a 'fifth column.'[6] Then there is the account, shortly to be quoted, of events at Chester only a decade later which describes the city as a very wealthy settlement. It is also considered the most likely location for the unidentified, prolific Mercian mint which began operation c.890 or possibly a little earlier and certainly a mint would not be established in a place unless it had a substantial population, significant economic activity and a degree of security.[7] Thus, while some of the population may well have fled at news of the Vikings' approach the term '*westre*' may refer to the ruins of the Roman fortress, the part most likely to have been occupied by the Danes, and not the entire settlement, which in all probability included a substantial community living close to the river south of the fortress. Viking armies in any case targeted places worthy of capture not deserted ruins.

Aethelred and his army reached Chester close on the heels of the Vikings and laid siege to it. They adopted a 'scorched earth' policy, seizing all the cattle in the area, gathering or burning all the corn available, and killing any Viking foragers. These tactics paid off and perhaps after only a few weeks the Viking army abandoned Chester and moved into North Wales. The following year it returned to the base at Mersea island via Northumbria rather than risk crossing hostile territory. Late in 894 the Vikings re-emerged and advanced by ship up the Thames and into the River Lea, where they set up a new base, possibly at Hertford. The English response the following summer involved several failed assaults, although the Viking fleet was successfully blockaded. While the English were busily engaged extending the siegeworks, the Danes made a break for it and managed to reach Bridgnorth on the River Severn, where they set up a new base. Despite surviving throughout the winter they withdrew the following year having failed to capture either land or booty and having lost all their ships. Some were so dispirited that they withdrew from England to seek new victims on the Continent.

The events of the late ninth century highlight the growing economic importance of Chester as well as its great strategic significance. Viking gains had reduced this part of Mercia to a narrow strip of territory lying between Danes

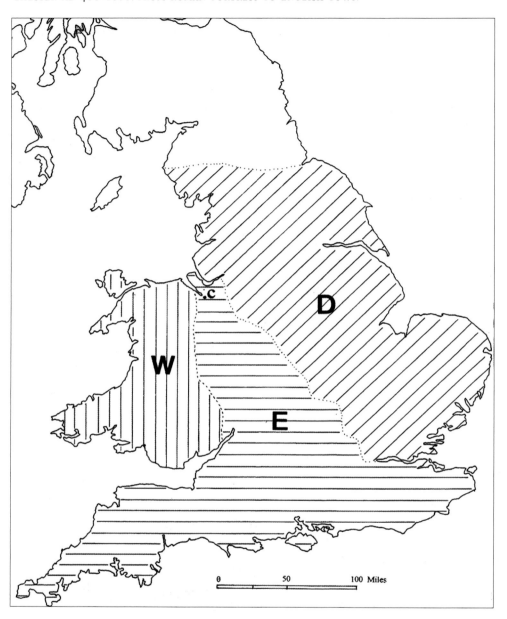

18 The extent of Viking conquest *c.*AD 890
Key: W – Wales, D – Danelaw, E – English territory

to the east and the not always friendly princedoms of Wales to the west. There was also the growing power of the Hiberno-Norse Vikings around the Irish Sea. Chester thus lay at the north-western tip of a wedge of English territory hedged in by no less than three either actively or potentially hostile powers. It possessed a sea-port that could function as a fleet base and also controlled access to the interior of Mercia via the Dee valley. Just as the Roman army centuries before had seized the area to prevent concerted action by the native tribes of the Pennines and North Wales, so the English came to recognise its value for hindering co-operation between the Danes of York and the Norse Vikings settled in Ireland (*18*).

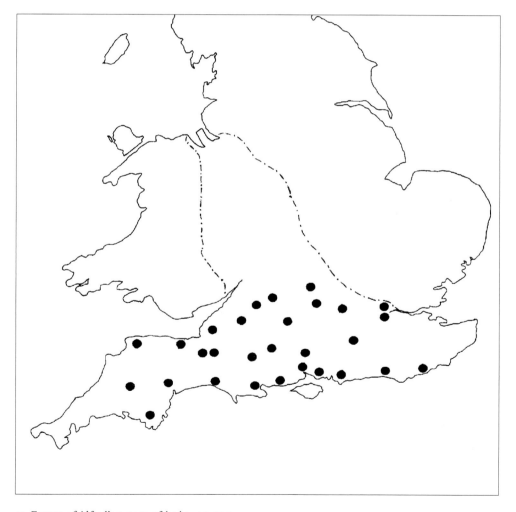

19 Extent of Alfred's system of *burhs* *c*.AD 900

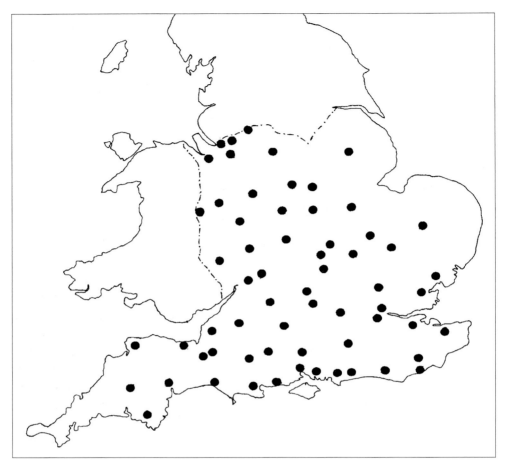

20 Re-conquest of Viking-held areas under Edward and Aetheflaed and extension of *burh* system by *c.*AD 920

While Alfred's work in Wessex laid the foundations for an English resurgence, much of the successful prosecution of the war against the Vikings was undertaken by Aethelred of Mercia. He gathered and led the forces necessary to pursue and contain the highly mobile Viking armies and, by employing a range of tactics including sieges as well as direct assault, succeeded in limiting their destructive potential. His strategic and tactical ability prevented the Vikings from either making any territorial gains or raiding freely. They were defeated on a number of occasions, suffering heavy casualties, the loss of their ships and the confiscation of their plunder. Alfred and Aethelred's military successes were based on two principal strategies, namely the reorganisation of the army coupled with the building of a network of fortresses known as *burhs*. The latter encompassed a variety of defended strongholds; some were purely military bases with modest garrisons while others were sizeable settlements with a large, resident civilian population. Thus, some were refurbished Roman forts, such as Portchester, while others were walled Roman towns, such as Chichester, Exeter and Winchester. Some were entirely new constructions, such as those at Hastings, Lewes and Wareham, while yet others were re-used Iron Age hillforts such as Chisbury, Halwell and, closer to home, Eddisbury. Although diverse in origin, type and size, they nonetheless provided a network of defended strongpoints which, begun in Wessex by Alfred and extended into Mercia by Aethelred and Alfred's successor Edward, meant that everyone was within 25 miles of a refuge to which they could retire when a Viking raiding-party was in the area (*19 & 20*)

Alfred also reorganised the *fyrd* service or *fyrdfaereld*, the ancient obligation on every free-born man to serve as a warrior when required by his lord. There was no permanent standing army; instead the men were assembled at the beginning of the campaigning season in those years when war was planned or anticipated and then sent home in late summer/early autumn ready to gather in the harvest. Alfred's innovation was to have one third of the army on garrison duty in the *burhs*, another third on active campaign, while the remainder tilled the land. In this way, he could take the battle to the enemy while at the same time protecting his own bases and also ensuring food production was maintained. Two other duties connected with military service were *burhbot* and *brycgbot* or *brycggeweorc*; that is, service in building bridges and service in repairing fortifications.[8] We hear an echo of this in the Domesday account of Chester, where it is stated that 'the shire-reeve (sheriff) was empowered to call out one man from every hide in Cheshire for the repair of the bridge and the wall of the city'.[9]

The Vikings' naval power was something else that Alfred sought to counter. He ordered the design and construction of a new type of longship. This was considerably larger than the average Viking ship, having up to 60 oars and a fighting complement twice the number. It was also, however, less agile and on a number of occasions the shallower draught of the Viking vessels enabled them to escape.

When Alfred died on 26 October 899 a succession crisis ensued which threatened to undo all that he and Aethelred had achieved. There were no firmly established rules on this matter in Wessex apart from the overall guiding principle that choosing the most competent adult male was more important than the continuation in power of any particular bloodline. Alfred named his elder son Edward as the main beneficiary in his will, but the throne was contested by Aethelwold, first son of Alfred's elder brother King Aethelred, who was older than Edward. Despite the recognition within Wessex that Edward's claim was the stronger, Aethelwold refused to accept this and sought support from the Danish kingdoms of East Anglia and Northumbria. He also recruited support within Mercia by encouraging an anti-Aethelred faction led by a certain Beorhtsige. Conflict ensued and matters came to a head with a battle at Holme in Huntingdonshire on 13 December 902. Although the Viking force was victorious, it was the end of Aethelwold's cause as he perished in the battle, along with Beorhtsige and the King of East Anglia.

The year 902 also witnessed an event that was to have considerable ramifications for the inhabitants of Chester and one that, despite the initially perilous circumstances, laid the foundations for its future prosperity:

> The Norsemen departed from Ireland and Ingimund was their leader and where they went to was the island of Britain. The king of Britain at this time was the brother of Cadell son of Rhodri. The men of Britain assembled against them and a hard, vigorous battle was given them, and they were driven by force from the territories of the men of Britain. Afterwards Ingimund with his forces came to Aethelflaed Queen of the Saxons, for her husband, that is Aethelraed was ill. Ingimund asked the Queen for land where he could settle and on which he would build huts and dwellings, for he was weary of war. Aethelflaed gave him lands near Chester (castra), and he stayed there for a time. When he saw the city full of wealth and the good land around it, he wanted to possess them. Then Ingimund came to the leaders of the Norsemen and Danes; he made a great complaint in their presence, and he said that they were poor without good land, and that it was right that they should seize Chester and take over its wealth and lands. Many great wars and battles occurred as a result. He said: 'Let us beseech and implore them first, and if we do not get them willingly in this way let us contest them by force'. All the leaders of the Norsemen and Danes agreed to this. Ingimund then went to his house, with an assembly following him. Though they made this council in secret, the queen came to know of it. Therefore the queen collected large forces around her in every direction, and the city of Chester was filled with her hosts.

> The armies of the Danes and Norsemen assembled towards Chester and, since they did not get their consent by beseeching or supplication, they proclaimed battle on a certain day. On that day they came to attack the city; there was a large force with many freemen in the city awaiting them. When the forces who were in the city saw, from the wall of the city, the great armies of the Danes and Norsemen approaching them, they sent messengers to the king of the Saxons, who was ill and at the point of death at that time, to ask his advice and the advice of the queen. This was the advice they gave: to make battle near the city outside, and the gate of the city should be wide open, and to choose a body of horsemen, concealed on the inside, and those of the people of the city who would be stronger in battle should flee back into the city as in defeat, and when the greater number of the forces of the Norsemen came inside the gate of the city the force hidden yonder should close the gate after this band and not admit any more; capture those who came into the city and kill

them all. This was all done accordingly, and complete slaughter was thus made of the Danes and the Norsemen. Great as that slaughter was however, the Norsemen did not abandon the city, for they were stubborn and vicious, but they all said that they would make many hurdles, and put posts under them, and pierce the wall under them. This was not delayed; the hurdles were made, and the forces were under them to pierce the wall, for they were eager to take the city to avenge their people.

Then the king and queen sent messengers to the Irishmen who were among the pagans to say to them 'Life and health to you from the king of the Saxons, and from his queen, who has all authority over the Saxons, and they are certain that you are true and trusty friends to them. Therefore, you should take their side; for they did not bestow greater honour on any Saxon warrior or cleric than they gave to each warrior and cleric who came to them from Ireland, because this inimical race of pagans is equally hostile to you also. It is right, then, for you, as trusty friends, to help them on this occasion. We have come from faithful friends of yours to address you so that you ask the Danes what tokens of lands and treasures they would give to those who would betray the city to them. If they accept this, bring them to a place to swear this where it will be easy to kill them; and when they are swearing by their swords and shields, as is their custom, they will lay aside all their missile weapons'. They all did this accordingly, and they put away their arms. And the reason why the Irishmen did this to the Danes was because they were less friends to them than to the Norsemen. Many of them were killed in this manner for large rocks and large beams were thrown down upon them; great numbers also by darts and spears and by every other means for killing man.
But the other forces, the Norsemen, were under the hurdles piercing the walls. What the Saxons and the Irishmen who were among them did was to throw down large rocks so that they destroyed the hurdles over them. What they did in the face of this was to place large posts under the hurdles. What the Saxons did was to put all the ale and water of the town in cauldrons, to boil them and pour them over those who were under the hurdles so that their skins were stripped from them. In response the Norsemen spread hides on the hurdles. What the Saxons did then was to let loose on the attacking force all the beehives of the town, so that they could not move their legs or hands from the great number of bees stinging them. Afterwards they left the city and abandoned it. It was not long after that [before they came] to wage battle again.

Annals of Ireland: translation by I.Ll. Foster in Wainwright 1942

The above extract is taken from an obscure Irish annalistic compilation which only survives as a copy of a manuscript which was itself copied from an earlier vellum manuscript in 1643.[10] Although in its existing form the story is obviously comparatively modern and embellished with literary flourishes it is nonetheless considered to be derived from part of a much earlier, and possibly contemporary, account. Material thought to derive from the same source occurs in the *Annals of Ulster* and the so-called *Annals of Tigernach*. The expulsion of the Vikings from Ireland is recorded in the first of these under the year 901, while the tenth-century Welsh chronicle known as the *Annales Cambriae* as well as the *Brut y Tywysogion* both refer to Ingimund by name and record his arrival on, and subsequent expulsion from, Anglesey. In addition, the description of Aethelflaed filling the city 'with her hosts' can be equated with the refortification of Chester recorded in the *Anglo-Saxon Chronicle sub anno* 907. Coins issued a few years later by the Chester mint bear an unusual series of pictorial designs, including one depicting a stone tower, a suitable symbol of the restored Roman fortress.

Discarding the literary embroidery of the various measures and counter-measures of the siege, the basics of the episode are clear: Norsemen, expelled from Ireland and repulsed from Anglesey, were given permission to settle on lands near Chester, most probably in the Wirral. After a period of peaceful co-existence the incomers became aggressive and began to cast envious eyes on Chester itself. Aethelflaed learned of their plans and sent forces to Chester to bolster its defence. A major attack on the city was launched by a force which included Irishmen, Danes and Norwegians. Despite its failure the besiegers renewed their efforts and so the Mercians tried, and apparently succeeded, in getting the Irish to change sides. The Danes were ambushed and the Norse attacks were eventually driven off, but further engagements followed. As to chronology, the expulsion of the Scandinavians took place in 902, while the refortification of Chester by Aethelflaed occurred in 907. According to the Irish Annals Aethelred was already ill when Ingimund was granted permission to settle near Chester. In other sources Aethelred's illness overtook him after his defeat of a large Viking force at the battle of Tettenhall on 5 August 910 and most probably stemmed from injuries sustained in that engagement. This seems likely from the fact that he died less than twelve months later. Taking the record of the Irish Annals at face value, Ingimund settled near Chester in the last months of Aethelred's reign. However, the *Anglo-Saxon Chronicle* records the refortification of Chester in 907, something which took place before the attack on the city. Most probably the assignment of Aethelred's illness to an earlier part of his reign was either an error or was employed to add an extra piece of drama to the story: a queen with an ill husband and under pressure from all sides granting land to barbarians. The attack on Chester is thus most likely to have occurred at some time in 910 or early the following year.

In view of Chester's undoubted strategic and probable economic importance the decision to allow Ingimund and his followers to settle close to the city could be seen as foolhardy. Subsequent events did indeed prove this to be so but, in fairness to Aethelred, Mercia had only just succeeded in fending off the threat from Aethelwold. The tactic of granting land to one group of barbarians under a treaty arrangement which obliged them to repel all further raiders or settlers – so common in the late Roman period – was one that had recently been employed on the Continent. There was, of course, the inherent risk in such arrangements that the settlers would turn on their hosts, just as Ingimund and his followers did.

Aethelred left no male heir and there were no close male relatives who could succeed him. The Lady Aethelflaed assumed the mantle of power, something very unusual in the Anglo-Saxon period and a testament both to her prestige and her abilities as a leader in a time of warfare. The need to preserve the recent and delicately balanced alliance with Wessex was no doubt another consideration on the part of those who could have altered the situation. For the remaining seven years of her life Aethelflaed led military campaigns in collaboration with King Edward. Mercian and West Saxon armies acted independently of one another but always in concert as complementary parts of a single military strategy. Viking armies occasionally achieved some initial success by surprise attacks, but the English forces gained victory after victory, gradually diminishing the area under Danish control. The army reforms introduced by Alfred bore fruit as the English were able to mount offensive operations while still retaining garrisons in the *burhs* sufficient to resist and repulse Viking attacks. The system of strongholds was extended. In our region *burhs* were founded at Bridgnorth in 912, at Tamworth and Stafford in 913, and at Eddisbury in 914 (*20*). This last provided a guard on Chester's flanks and was well sited to intercept any Viking force erupting from Northumbria along the old Roman road from Manchester to Chester. Others followed in 915 at the unlocated site of *Weardbyrig* (possibly Gwespyr, near Llanasa, in Clwyd) and Runcorn, designed to control access up the river systems of the Dee and Mersey respectively. In 916 Aethelflaed sent an army further into Wales and took prisoner the Queen of Brecon and many of the regal entourage, extracting a substantial ransom for their release. The following year she launched her first offensive into Danish-occupied territory and captured the Viking fortress at Derby. The East Anglian Vikings launched a counter-offensive against Edward but were defeated and their king slain. The following year Lady Aethelflaed took the fortress at Leicester but she died soon afterwards. Following her death Edward became ruler of Mercia and Wessex and soon received oaths of allegiance not only from the Welsh kingdoms, like Aethelflaed before him, but also from the rulers of Bamburgh, Strathclyde, York and the Scots.

Edward was operating in northern Mercia in 919-20, establishing *burhs* at Thelwell, Manchester and Bakewell. His ordering of the construction of a *burh* at Rhuddlan in 921 appears to have upset the Welsh, who rose in revolt. Chester, too, sided with the rebels; its mixed population of Mercians, Welsh, Norse and Irish perhaps discontented with direct rule from Wessex. Edward was forced to come north in person to quell the revolt late in either 923 or 924. This was one of his last actions, for he died in July 924 at Farndon. In view of the recent troubles this is perhaps more likely to have been the Cheshire rather than the Nottinghamshire Farndon. Two years later, Edward's successor Athelstan managed to seize York and all England was brought under the sway of Wessex. The acquisition of the Danish-occupied areas of England, with their strong tradition of ship-building and seafaring, as well as ready-made fleets, may explain the sudden growth of English naval power under Aethelstan. In 934 he launched an invasion of Scotland by land and sea and soon received the submission of King Constantine. Three Welsh kings, Hywel Dda of Deheubarth, Morgan of Gwent and Idwal of Gwynedd, were present in Athelstan's expeditionary force, indicating that the dues they owed to the King of Wessex included the supply of troops for his campaigns. William of Malmesbury's much later account states that North Wales also had to pay an annual tribute of 20 pounds of gold, 300 pounds of silver, 25,000 oxen, hounds and hawks. Yet the Welsh kings stayed loyal to Athelstan when his enemies conspired against him a few years later, so presumably they shared in the spoils of his campaigns. The simmering resentment felt by the Scandinavians and those in the native kingdoms of the north came to the boil in 937 when the Vikings of Northumbria, aided by their kin from Dublin and joined by the Kings of Strathclyde and the Scots, moved against Athelstan. The two sides met at *Brunanburh*, where the Vikings and their allies were soundly beaten. The location of the battle site is still debated although Bromborough, dismissed by some, still seems a likely candidate.[11]

Athelstan died in 939 and was succeeded by his son Edmund. The hold of Wessex on the north was beginning to weaken, to the extent that Edmund had to recapture the Anglo-Danish *burhs* of the Midlands. The Welsh, too, tried to cast off their allegiance to Wessex with the consequence that Edmund was forced to campaign in North Wales where he defeated and killed Idwal of Gwynedd in 943, leaving Hywel Dda as sole ruler. Edmund was murdered in 946 and succeeded by his brother Eadred, whose reign was largely spent subduing the rebellious kingdom of York. Eadred was in his turn replaced by Edmund's elder son Eadwig. The latter was challenged by his younger brother Edgar, who quickly gained sufficient support to take control of both Mercia and Northumbria. Eadwig died in 959 and Edgar then added Wessex to his domain. It was during his 16-year reign that the process of integrating Mercia and Northumbria into a single kingdom with Wessex reached its culmination and the point at which the story of England really began.

Edgar bestowed benefactions on the areas that had originally supported him and Chester features prominently in his reign. He granted a charter to St Werburgh's abbey in 958 which gave it various estates around Chester. He in fact granted seventeen hides of land to the abbey 'in diverse scattered places'.[12]

This description suggests the donation of land in parcels detached from several royal estates and implies the existence of extensive royal land in the area. Edgar's coronation, curiously delayed, took place at Bath in 973. Soon afterwards, he sailed north to Chester with a large fleet, where he received homage from a number of subject kings; the *Anglo-Saxon Chronicle* says six, while Florence of Worcester states there were eight, as does Higden's later *Polychronicon*. Florence's is the fullest account:

> Thence, after a short time, he sailed round the north part of Britain with a large fleet, and landed at Chester. Eight petty kings, namely, Malcolm, king of the Cumbrians, Kynarth, king of the Scots, Maccus, king of the Isles, and five others, named Dufnall, Siferth, Huwall, Jakob and Juchill, met hime there as he had appointed, and swore that they would be faithful to him, and assist him by land and by sea. On a certain day they attended him into a boat, and when he had placed them at the oars, he himself took the helm and skilfully steered it down the river Dee, and thus, followed by the whole company of earls and nobles, in this order went from the palace to the monastery of St John the Baptist. After having prayed there, he returned with same pomp to the palace. As he was entering it, he is reported to have said to his nobles, that when his successors might boast themselves to be kings of the English, when, attended by so many kings, they should enjoy the pomp of such honours.

The location of Edgar's palace is unknown. Thorpe, quoted above, translated the Latin as 'down' but it could equally well have meant 'along'. The spot known as Edgar's Field, which lies immediately west of the south end of the Old Dee Bridge, is traditionally held to have been the site of Edgar's residence, but there is no proof of this. Had it been sited there, then the voyage must have taken place at high tide so that the vessel could clear the rock bar where the later weir was constructed. Others have suggested there was a royal estate at Farndon (with its centre and thus possibly a palace at Aldford), but the reference in the Chronicle may have been to the Farndon in Nottinghamshire.[14] Would Edgar really have inflicted the five-mile row from Aldford to St John's on his allies? A shorter journey would surely have sufficed for a symbolic demonstration of their allegiance. There is also the matter of the difficulties the 'whole company of earls and nobles' would have experienced in keeping up with the vessel, given the valleys and marshlands which disrupt both banks of the Dee. Perhaps, therefore, Edgar's palace was nearer to Chester. Indeed, the king and his retinue are most likely to have resided in the city itself, close to his fleet and in the place of maximum security. As to the event at St John's, one can well imagine that the formal ceremonies in the monastery church were followed by popular celebrations and feasting outside, perhaps located in the neighbouring amphitheatre which, although somewhat ruinous, would still have provided a usable venue.

Edgar's visit marked something of a high point in the *burh*'s fortunes, with the city honoured by the presence of the monarch with all his retinue and military might, and its population witnessing eight other rulers pledging their allegiance to him. It must have been a time of great feasting as well as a stirring spectacle for the people of Chester. Unfortunately, more troubled times lay ahead, but before moving on to describe the fortunes of the city in the century preceding the Norman Conquest we shall first examine the archaeological evidence for the rejuvenated Chester of the tenth century.

VI

THE BURH IN DETAIL

DEFENCES AND THE DEFENDED AREA

Precisely how and when the defences of the Roman legionary fortress were extended to encompass the much larger area enclosed by the medieval city walls are questions for which definitive answers have still to be found. There are, however, some facts available which narrow the time-frame for this transition. Clearly, the refortification of Chester by Aethelflaed is the earliest date when any major work to the defences can feasibly have been undertaken. A *terminus ante quem* is given by documentary sources which confirm that the city walls as we know them existed by the mid-twelfth century and that the churches constructed on the sites of the south and west gates of the Roman fortress (St Michael's and Holy Trinity respectively) had also been built by this time.[1] Thus, the limits of the period within which the defences were extended can be fixed as 907-*c*.1150. There are though further possible complications; for example, the expansion may have occurred in a series of separate stages rather than as a single event; also, the legionary defences could have been retained alongside any new additions (*21*; for an artist's impression of the *burh* in the later tenth century see *colour plate 26*).

It follows from this that we cannot at present define beyond doubt the course taken by, and thus the size of the area enclosed within, the defences of the *burh* as originally founded, nor indeed the form of its defences. However, by piecing together various items of evidence – both historical and archaeological – it is possible to suggest a plausible sequence of development. Beginning with the historical evidence, the Chester monk Henry Bradshaw in his *Life of St Werburgh*, written in the late fifteenth century, says, recounting the achievements of the Lady Aethelflaed:

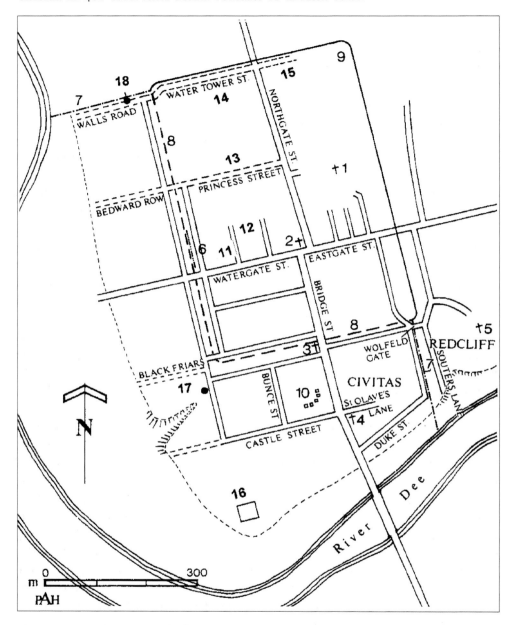

21 Chester. Plan of the *burh*
Key: Pre-Conquest churches: 1 – St Werburgh's, 2 – St Peter's, 3 – St Bridget's, 4 – St Olave's,
5 – St John's; 6 – possible re-ue of Roman fortress defences (Linenhall Street); 7 – possible extensions to
Roman fortress wall when *burh* created; 8 – line of Roman fortress wall; 9 – Roman fortress defences
continue in use; excavated Anglo-Saxon structures: 10 – Lower Bridge Street (west), 11 – Crook Street,
12 – Hamilton Place, 13 – Princess Street, 14 – Northgate Brewery, 15 – Abbey Green; 16 – site of
Norman castle; findspots of coin/bullion hoard: 17 – Castle Esplanade, 18 – Pemberton's Parlour

Also she enlarged this sayde olde cite
With new myghty walles stronge all about
Almost by proportion double in quantite
To the farther byldynge brought without doubt
She compassed in the castell enemies to hold out
Within the sayd walles to defend the towne
Agaynst the Danes and Walshemen to dryve them downe.

(Hawkins ed. 1848, 157)

The area of the medieval walled town was twice that of the fortress (130 versus 60 acres) and by ascribing a doubling of the walled area to Aethelflaed he is implying that it was during her time that the line of the present walls was established. This is also implied by the reference to the inclusion of the castle, even though it was not built until 160 years after the foundation of the *burh*. The mention of 'new myghty walles' also implies that the extended defences were constructed of masonry. We do not know what evidence, if any, Bradshaw had for stating it was Aethelflaed who extended the defended area.

A second, and rather more reliable, piece of evidence is contained in the Domesday Survey, which reveals that the line of the city wall running from the south-east angle of the Roman fortress down to the river had for some time marked the boundary between the city and the neighbouring hundred.[2] Thirdly, we have information contained in the tenth-century document known as the *Burghal Hidage*. Referring to the situation in Wessex it states that each hide of land assigned to a *burh* was required to provide one man for the maintenance of its defences and that each pole (5½yds or 5.03m) of wall required four men to defend it.[3] In many cases where the full circuit of defences is known, the *Burghal Hidage* assessment is in close agreement with the actual length of fortification. In others, the assessment and length of defences agree when sectors of the circuit formed by a natural obstacle such as a river are omitted. It is very likely that the same formula was applied in Mercia, especially as the Domesday account of Chester contains an entry which reads 'For the maintenance of the city wall and bridge the reeve used to call out one man from each hide in the County'.[4] Cheshire was almost certainly assessed at 1,200 hides and so, applying the formula, this gives a length for the *burh* defences of *c.*1,500m, or a little less if allowance is made for the bridge. This is significantly short of the total perimeter of the fortress circuit which was *c.*2,000m. However, if one assumes the *burh* defences were formed by extending the north and east walls of the Roman fortress down to the river along the line taken by the medieval walls, then the total length omitting the river frontage would be *c.*1,400m; very close to the figure suggested by the *Burghal Hidage* formula and leaving a force of around 100 men assigned to the defence of the bridge. While in this scheme the total area enclosed was greater than that of the fortress, extending the old Roman defences down to the river to create an inverted L-shape fortification significantly reduced the length of landward defences needing to be manned and thus was more efficient in terms of manpower. Although this is a neat solution on paper, does the archaeological evidence support it?

It might be easier to answer that question had any archaeological investigation taken place on those stretches of the city walls running from the relevant Roman angle-towers down to the river. Circumstances have never permitted or required this so evidence obtained from sites on other parts of the defences will have to be deployed. The results of an excavation on the fortress defences a little north of the west gate in 1961-2 (Linenhall Street site) might, at first sight, appear to contradict the theory. Here, cut into the top of the fortress rampart and themselves cut by thirteenth- and fourteenth-century pits, was a series of massive post-pits linked by a narrow trench (22). These features were convincingly interpreted as the emplacement for a substantial palisade supported by large vertical posts representing a post-Roman refurbishment of the fortress defences, attributed, in the absence of any dating evidence, to the period of the *burh*'s creation.[5] However, even if the suggested dating is correct, this does not necessarily rule out the notion of an extension of the defences down to the river. Carrington proposed that there may have been a system comprising an inner and outer enceinte, the inner consisting of the patched-up fortress defences and the outer of 'spur' ramparts on the line of the later medieval extensions.[6] Such a patching of the defences could, of course, have taken place on any number of previous occasions; the temporary occupation by the Viking army in 893 being one that readily springs to mind.

It is appropriate at this juncture to consider the Roman defences in greater detail. It has long been known that extensive lengths of the curtain wall were rebuilt at some point in their history and that numerous fragments of inscribed tombstones and larger funerary monuments were reused as core material in this reconstruction.[7] This fact first came to light during repairs to the north wall in the late nineteenth century, when it was discovered that almost the entire stretch of wall west of the Northgate had been rebuilt in this fashion, along with some parts of the sector east of the gate.[8] In addition to being less extensive the repair work east of the gate differed from that to the west in that here the wall was rebuilt to more than twice the thickness of the primary wall, whereas on the west the original width of 1.5m was maintained. Photographs of the latter show that although the general style of the original fortress wall – with its large facing-blocks and a projecting chamfered plinth just above the base course – the blocks, and thus the courses of masonry, were taller than those employed in the

22 Palisade trench and post-pits cut
into top of rampart of Roman defences.
Linenhall Street 1963-4 excavation.
© *Chester Archaeological Society*

late first-/early second-century wall, giving it a much 'chunkier' appearance.
Also, the courses varied in height and the quality of the finishing of the stone
– much of which must have been freshly quarried despite the recycling of earlier
material – was inferior to the earlier workmanship.

Excavations on the west defences in the twentieth century found further
evidence of rebuilding incorporating similar reused material. The stretch running
between the west gate and the first interval tower to the north had been rebuilt
to the 'broad gauge,' while a lengthy section of that south of the gate had been
reconstructed adhering to the original specification.[9] In all of these cases, the
occurrence of reused stonework in the footing course of the wall proved that the
rebuilding was extremely thorough and not merely a superficial refurbishment.
Similarly, the employment of two different specifications in the rebuilding
implies – in the absence of any other obvious reason – two different periods of
work.

The date of these reconstructions has been much debated over the years. In
the decades following the discoveries on the north wall, dates ranging from

the late Roman period to the immediate aftermath of the English Civil War were proposed. With the revelation in the 1960s that parts of the west wall of the fortress had also been rebuilt incorporating funerary memorials it became clear that some at least of this reconstruction work must pre-date the twelfth century, the time when the south and west walls finally became redundant. An opportunity to review the evidence in print once more came in the form of a publication reporting on archaeological observations made during a programme of repair and stabilisation works to the north wall and the northern sector of the east wall at the end of the twentieth century. The author, Charles LeQuesne, came to the conclusion that the rebuilding of the fortress wall most probably occurred at the time of the *burh*'s creation in 907, reasoning that it was unthinkable that the defences could have fallen into a state where they required such extensive reconstruction within the Roman period.[10]

However, that this is precisely what did happen is indicated by the evidence from an excavation on the east defences in 1988-9. The site in question, formerly occupied by the public library, lay on the west side of St John Street, situated mid-way between the fortress east gate and the south-east angle.[11] Excavation of the fortress ditch showed that it had been allowed to silt up completely, even filling in the rain-drip channel on the basal course of the curtain wall. The extent and duration of this neglect can be appreciated from the fact that the ditch was approximately 7m wide and in excess of 3m deep. Eventually, the area was tidied up by the laying down of a 30cm-thick surfacing of compacted sandstone rubble which sealed the ditch and ran up to the face of the fortress wall. There was a distinct change in the character of the latter at the level of the fourth course above the chamfered plinth where the backing material changed from mortar to clay. This suggested a rebuilding, an impression reinforced by the fact that a block with mouldings imported from elsewhere was present in the fourth course. Furthermore, sunk into the soft fill of the ditch and sealed by the sandstone surfacing was a mass of heavy rubble which included damaged facing-blocks from the fortress wall. Clearly, either part of the wall had collapsed and/or this material had been discarded during the dismantling and rebuilding process.[12]

The few sherds of pottery recovered from the sandstone surfacing and the layer immediately above it belonged to the late third or early fourth century.[13] The quantity of material is so small that no great reliance can be placed upon it for dating purposes and it would be a legitimate premise to suppose it got there at a much later date and that the rebuilding of the wall here was part of the Aethelflaedan refortification of Chester. However, the subsequent sequence of events on the site demonstrates that this cannot have been the case. Over a period of time the rebuilt fortress wall began to tilt outwards at an ever-increasing angle, a process dramatically attested by the numerous pressure fractures on the faces

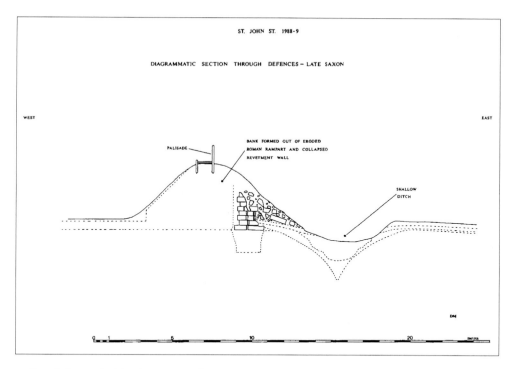

23 East defences, St John Street 1989, diagrammatic section showing collapsed Roman fortress wall and possible form of tenth-century refurbished defences. © *Chester Archaeological Society*

of the facing-blocks in the wall's lower courses (*5*). Eventually, the wall collapsed forming, together with tumbled material from the rampart behind it, a low mound of rubble and soil. Evidence recovered in 1973 from a spot 25m to the south suggests this collapse affected a substantial length of the fortress wall. Subsequently, the outer part of this mound was dug away for the creation of a ditch. This was presumably defensive and as such is likely to have been accompanied by some other feature such as a palisade or breastwork set atop the crest of the mound some distance back from the line of the buried Roman wall (*23*). The ditch could not be dated precisely but was considerably earlier than a lime-kiln associated with the building of the city wall in the twelfth century.

The obliteration of the fortress wall explains why in this sector the medieval wall is set back 3-4m from its Roman predecessor, whereas in the other sectors where the medieval and Roman defences follow the same line one stands almost directly atop the other. Clearly, the rebuilding of the fortress wall cannot be Aethelflaedan; the timespan available simply is not long enough to accommodate this sequence of events, nor is such a sequence likely given the circumstances of the period. Rather, the evidence of the pottery recovered from the surfacing in front of the wall should be taken at face value and the rebuilding of the fortress wall attributed to the opening decades of the fourth century. The ditch subsequently cut through the debris of its collapse would thus represent the Aethelflaedan refortification. Even without the evidence of the St John Street excavation one must in any case seriously doubt whether Aethelflaed would have had a workforce at her disposal large enough, and possessing the requisite skills, to rebuild more than 1,000m of fortress wall from ground level to a standard approaching that of the Roman masons and requiring much freshly quarried stone. We should also remember that Aethelflaed refortified Chester in an emergency situation, circumstances hardly appropriate for an enterprise that would have taken years to complete.

In summary, therefore, the works undertaken to make Chester defensible at the time of the *burh*'s creation most probably consisted of relatively minor and easily completed works consisting of repairs to the Roman fortifications where they still survived largely intact along with the closing up of breaches with a timber palisade where the curtain wall was more ruinous. The example of the latter found at the Linenhall Street site suggests that the entire fortress circuit was refurbished and this might well have been a sensible precaution even if, as seems very likely, lengths of earth rampart were also constructed at the same time to extend the defences down to the river from the north-west and south-east angles.[14]

STREET PLAN

As far as can be discerned, the street plan of the medieval city still largely in evidence today already existed by the eleventh century. Indeed, analogy with other *burhs* suggests that this was probably established when Chester was refounded in 907. As in many other places of Roman origin a street grid already existed and, again like those other places, some elements of this continued in use, others were discarded while, in a few cases, new ones were created. Unsurprisingly, the major streets of the Chester *burh* were essentially the principal ones of the Roman fortress. Their re-use was guaranteed by the fact that the only major breaches of the defences continued to be the gatehouses of the old fortress, no matter whether still standing or largely ruinous. Thus, the *via praetoria* became Bridge Street while the eastern and western sectors of the *via principalis* evolved into Eastgate Street and Watergate Street respectively. As mentioned above, there were minor changes of alignment between the original and the new courses of the *via principalis* which may have been caused by the blocking of one of the portals at both gates; the southern at the east gate and the northern at the west

1 Legionary bath-building. Layer of 'dark earth' covering floor of one of the main bathing-halls sealed by debris of collapsed roof-vault. © *Chester City Council*

2 Aerial view of Heronbridge earthwork, taken 1985. © *Chesire County Council*

Above: 3 Heronbridge today. Rampart and ditch at south end of seventh-century fort

Left: 4 Heronbridge 2004. Rows of skeletons in mass-grave

5 Heronbridge 2004. Two skeletons selected for removal under excavation

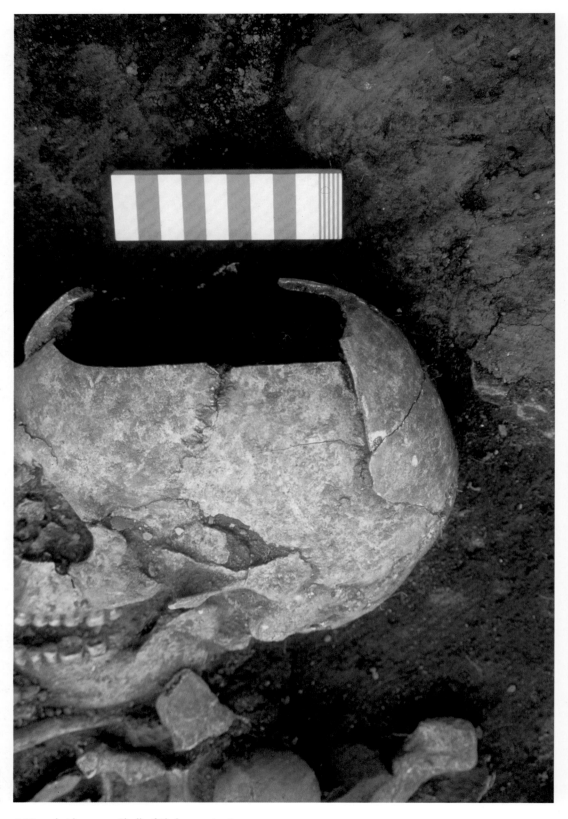

6 Heronbridge 2004. Skull of Skeleton 1 in situ

7 Heronbridge 2004. Skull of skeleton left in situ

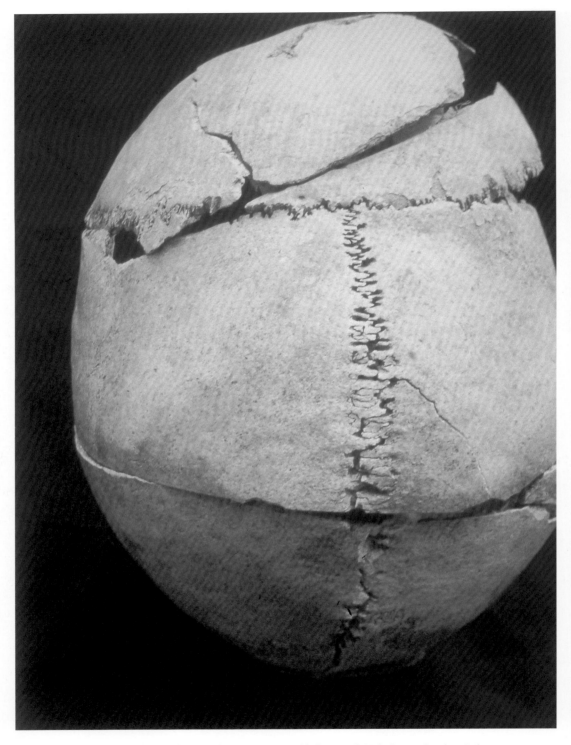

8 Heronbridge 2004. Skull of Skeleton 2 showing weapon–blade cuts. © *York Osteoarchaeology Ltd*

Above: 9 Heronbridge 2004.
Skull of Skeleton 2. Close-up
of weapon-blade cuts. © *York
Osteoarchaeology Ltd*

Right: 10 Heronbridge 2004.
Weapon-blade cut on right
cheek-bone of Skeleton 2.
© *York Osteoarchaeology Ltd*

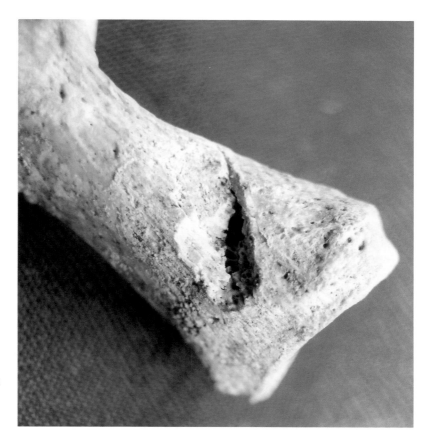

Right: 13 Heronbridge 2004. Defensive injury on thumb-bone of Skeleton 1. © *York Osteoarchaeology Ltd*

Above: 14 Heronbridge 2004. Forehead of Skeleton 1 showing healed depression fractures from previous injury. © *York Osteoarchaeology Ltd*

Right: 15 Heronbridge 2004. Skeleton 1. Dental abscess. © *York Osteoarchaeology Ltd*

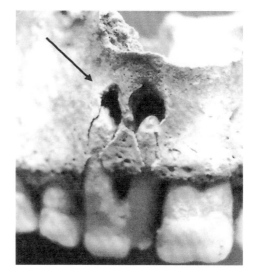

Opposite above: 11 Heronbridge 2004. Skull of Skeleton 1 showing weapon-blade cuts. © *York Osteoarchaeology Ltd*

Opposite below: 12 Heronbridge 2004. Skull of Skeleton 1 showing cuts at right ear. © *York Osteoarchaeology Ltd*

16 Heronbridge 2002. Section through northern defences of seventh-century fort showing remains of collapsed stone revetment at front of rampart

Above: 17 Heronbridge 2004. Section through
defences of seventh-century fort near middle of
west side showing dark and organically rich fill
of ditch sealed by thick deposit of clay associated
with late medieval slighting of defences

Right: 18 Heronbridge 2004. Section through
defences of seventh-century fort near middle of
west side showing blocks of stone from frontal
rampart revetment re-used to form floor of later
flax-retting tank constructed in bottom of its
ditch

Above: 19 Heronbridge 2004.
Close-up of preserved stalks of
flax plants found in ditch-fill of
seventh-century fort

Left: 20 Ninth-century silver
disc-brooch found during Lower
Bridge Street (west) excavation
1974. © *Chester City Council*

Opposite above: 21 Abbey Green
excavation 1975-8. Tenth-century
gravel road. © *Chester City
Council*

Opposite below: 22 Lower Bridge
Street (west) excavation 1974-6.
Remains of rock-cut cellar of
tenth-century building. Building
1 looking east. Note line of
internal post-settings opposite
entrance which was just outside
picture at bottom left. © *Chester
City Council*

Left: 23 Lower Bridge Street (west) excavation 1974-6. Remains of semi-sunken interior of tenth-century building – Building 4. © *Chester City Council*

Below: 24 Abbey Green excavation 1975-8. Corn-drying oven. © *Chester City Council*

Above: 25 Abbey Green excavation 1975–8. Antler-soaking pit. © *Chester City Council*

Below: 26 Reconstruction painting of the Chester *burh* as it may have appeared in late tenth century. The view is towards the north-east. Evidence recovered since this printing was done suggests there was probably more development along the main street frontages by this period. © *Chester City Council*

27 Complete Chester-
ware pot, Hunter Street
School excavation
1979-81. © *Chester City
Council*

28 View showing northern half of amphitheatre with St John's Church in the background. © *Chester City Council*

gate. The fourth major street of the Roman fortress was the *via decumana*, which was a relatively short thoroughfare running from the north gate roughly as far as the spot where the north end of the Market Square now stands. The space between this spot and the *via principalis* was occupied by two large buildings, the southern one being the headquarters building, and so the *via decumana* split into two minor streets running down the east and west sides. By the twelfth century the line of the *via decumana* had been extended southwards across the sites of the Roman buildings. This followed a slightly diagonal route so that by the time it reached Eastgate Street it ran only a little to the west of its Roman predecessor. Excavation of the Hunter's Walk site in 1979-80 showed that the Roman street on the west side of the building behind the *principia* may have been re-used in the Anglo-Saxon period but had been built over by the eleventh century. It seems likely, therefore, that the creation of a direct route from the north gate to Eastgate Street occurred either at the time of the *burh*'s foundation or not long afterwards.

An essential feature of Roman fort design was the street that ran around the entire perimeter immediately behind the defences, the so-called *via sagularis*. To some extent this was copied by those who laid out the *burhs*, enabling easy access to the defences and serving to connect the ends of lanes stretching back from the main streets.[15] In some areas of Chester the line of the *via sagularis* persisted through the Middle Ages to become part of the modern street plan. Thus in the western half of the fortress area its line is preserved by Whitefriars, Weaver Street (originally Alvin's or Bereward's Lane) and Trinity Street. Beyond the latter street's junction with Princess Street (Parsons Lane) there are no streets to perpetuate its course and this is true of the rest of the fortress defensive circuit apart from Water Tower Street, running inside the western half of the northern fortress defences. The last-named street is a comparatively modern addition to the city's street system. However, excavations on the Northgate Brewery site in 1972-3 revealed a stretch of gravelling overlying the *via sagularis* at a higher level which might represent the remains of a late Anglo-Saxon successor.[16] This possibility is strengthened by the fact that a far more substantial length of tenth-century street was found above the *via sagularis* on the Abbey Green site east of the north gate a few years later (*colour plate 21*).[17] The Roman street here was buried beneath a considerable accumulation of soil, so it is clear that this later street was an entirely new creation, not simply a re-using of the ancient thoroughfare. The presence of sherds of Chester ware pottery in the layers immediately beneath it show that it was laid down several decades after the *burh*'s creation. A spread of gravel surfacing found on the Bell Tower site in 1971 suggests that this putative intramural street also continued down the eastern defences, while a similar feature found beside the eastern section of the southern defences in 1955 would complete the circuit. There seems every possibility therefore that the Roman *via sagularis* was re-established in its entirety in the early days of the *burh* and that, for whatever reasons, elements of it were subsequently abandoned. In the north-east quarter of the fortress area this is probably to be explained by St Werburgh's Abbey taking direct control and restricting secular activity to the Northgate Street frontage at the western margin of its land-holding. If, as was argued above, the creation of the *burh* saw the building of extensions from the north-west and south-east corners of the Roman defences to make Chester a promontory fort, then this is likely to have been accompanied by the laying down of an intramural street along the lines followed by modern Water Tower Street and Park Street.

The existence of streets perpetuating the line of the *via sagularis* on the south and west sides of the fortress obviously implies that the Roman rampart and curtain wall were still a major feature of the landscape during the early phases of the *burh*'s existence, although this does not necessarily mean they still functioned as defences. A similar pattern of replication is discernible in the history of the road or patrol track that once ran round the fortress immediately beyond its defensive ditch. On the south its line is perpetuated by Pepper Street and Cuppin Street (Copines Lane); on the west by Nicholas Street (St Nicholas's Lane) and St Martin's Way (Crofts Lane); on the north by Dee Lane and Delamere Street; and on the east by Frodsham Street (Cow Lane) and St John's Street (Ironmongers Lane). The fact that this 'extramural' street runs close to and parallel with the re-established *via sagularis* on the south and west sides of the fortress might indicate that it, too, belongs to this early period.

Many of the minor streets of the fortress interior did not survive to become incorporated in the *burh* street system. The majority of these, such as the ones running between barrack blocks, were irrelevant and served no purpose. A few, however, were brought back into use, although the choice of line was perhaps influenced more by a break in the mounds of rubble left by the collapsed Roman buildings rather than definite knowledge of an ancient route. Crook Street (earlier Gerard's Lane), running north from Watergate Street, has been shown by excavation to be a tenth-century recommissioning of a street running between barracks of the First Cohort.[18] Its course beyond modern Hamilton Place followed the line of the Roman street which separated the principal fortress workshops from the Elliptical Building. Hamilton Place – itself the original Crook Street, or rather Crokes Lane – ran from Crook Street eastwards to Northgate Street and followed the line of the Roman street which ran along the north end of the First Cohort barracks and the rear of the headquarters building. The personal name Crok is derived from Old Norse *Krokr* and perhaps indicates that *Crokes Lane* was already in existence by the later tenth or early eleventh century, when Scandinavian influence in the city was at its height.

Further north, Princess Street, Hunter Street and King Street are all thought to be of post-Conquest date.

The creation of something approaching a regular street-grid in other *burhs* allows a few other possible candidates to be identified. Goss Street, mid-way between Crook Street and Northgate Street, is one, while St Werburgh's Lane, which linked the abbey with Eastgate Street, is another. There is some evidence (see below) to suggest that Goss Street once continued northwards as far as Princess Street, re-establishing the line of the street which ran down the west side of the enormous building which lay behind the *principia*. Directly opposite the south end of St Werburgh's Lane lay Newgate Street, formerly Fleshmongers' Lane. This cut through the line of the southern fortress defences and then curved sharply eastwards to pass through the Wolf Gate (now the Newgate). If the suggestion is accepted that the extension of the *burh* defences down to the river occurred before the Conquest then Newgate Street probably originated in the tenth century. It was most probably the site of the eight houses mentioned in Domesday as belonging to St John's and lying within the city.[19]

Park Street runs immediately behind the stretch of the city walls from the south-east angle of the fortress down to the river and, if pre-Conquest, would constitute a further example of a *burh via sagularis*. It formed a continuation of Duke Street (originally Claverton Lane), which itself ran parallel with the river to join Lower Bridge Street. It was probably somewhere along Duke Street that the eight burgages recorded in Domesday as lying '*in civitate*' and belonging to the manor of Claverton were situated. A little to the north of Duke Street lies St Olave's (originally St Olaf's) Lane. This route's alignment, like that of Castle Street directly opposite to it on the other side of Lower Bridge Street, runs parallel with the southern fortress defences and both seem very likely to belong to the pre-Conquest burghal street-grid. In the case of Castle Street this notion receives indirect support from the layout of the tenth-century buildings found to the north of it in the 1970s. As regards St Olave's Lane, this takes its name from the church of St Olaf which stands on the south side of its junction with Lower Bridge Street. This was very probably established soon after the death of King Olaf in 1030.

East of the fortress the road issuing from the east gate (now Foregate Street) continued in use, now becoming the main approach to the city from the east and south. In the Domesday survey the 'bishop's borough' – equivalent to the parish of St John's – contained 56 houses and some of these most probably lay along Foregate Street. Of the areas immediately outside the defences this is the one where extramural occupation is first likely to have developed because of its commercial potential, replicating the situation of the Roman period when it lay at the heart of the trading quarter of the *canabae*. At the southern end of St John

Street the Roman road skirting around the northern half of the amphitheatre afforded a ready made route to St John's Church. Although the street system in this area today has a strong east–west bias, historically, the principal axis of communication was north–south, connecting the commercial quarter along Foregate Street with the river frontage at the lower end of Souters Lane. There may well have been quays here used by river traffic. It was also somewhere near here that King Edgar and the sub-kings who crewed the royal barge disembarked in 973 on their way to St John's.

BUILDINGS AND BUILDING-TYPES

Apart from churches and their associated ecclesiastical buildings, the dwellings and other structures of the pre-Norman population would have been constructed of timber. Leaving little trace in the ground, it is understandable therefore why their remains can be difficult to recognise in the often confined conditions of urban excavation. It is also true to say that it was not until the 1970s, with the advent of large-scale area excavation and circumstances which enabled the search for such remains to be accorded a higher priority, that real advances in our understanding were made. Thus, before 1974, not a single building of the Anglo-Saxon era was known in Chester, yet within a decade excavations were to reveal more than twenty buildings dating to the tenth and eleventh centuries and representing a range of types and sizes.

The first buildings to be identified were revealed by the 1974-6 excavations to the west of Lower Bridge Street, in the area defined by Bunce Street, Castle Street and Grosvenor Place.[20] Here, the remains of no fewer than five rectangular timber buildings were found belonging to a planned scheme of development implemented at some time in the first half of the tenth century (23-29 and colour plates 22 & 23). The buildings were laid out in a reversed L-shape running roughly parallel with Lower Bridge Street and Castle Street, one arm 20m back from the former and the other 30m back from the latter. Had excavation of a greater area been possible this may well have revealed further buildings forming a square or rectangular layout arranged around a central 'courtyard'. The buildings investigated were spaced at intervals of 3-4m, a distribution which suggests a sixth building lay in the portion of the eastern arm unavailable for excavation.

Sufficient of four of the buildings was excavated to show that they had very similar dimensions, approximating to a standard size of 4.05 x 5.10m (possibly 12 x 16ft based on the Northern rod of 16.5 modern feet).[21] The westernmost building in the southern arm (Building 5) was ground-based with its main vertical wall-posts set in individual post-pits. Only a small portion of this building was explored

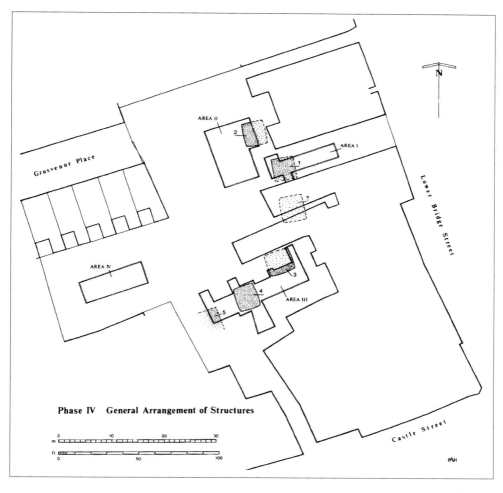

24 Lower Bridge Street (west) 1974-6. Plan showing layout of tenth-century buildings.
© *Chester City Council*

and it had been severely damaged by later occupation. Its neighbour to the east
(Building 4) was semi-sunken; that is its floor lay 0.80m below external ground
level. Here the wall-posts were set in shallow locating-holes excavated into the
solid rock around the perimeter of the floor area. Preparations for the erection of
Building 4 had got as far as the excavation of the locating-holes on three sides of
the floor area when the decision was made to enlarge it northwards, increasing its
north–south dimension to 6.80m. Buildings 1–3 formed a third category in that
they were equipped with full cellars averaging 1.80m in depth and cut into solid
sandstone bedrock. As in Building 4, the wall-posts (five or six per side) were set
in locating-holes positioned around the edge of the cellar floor.

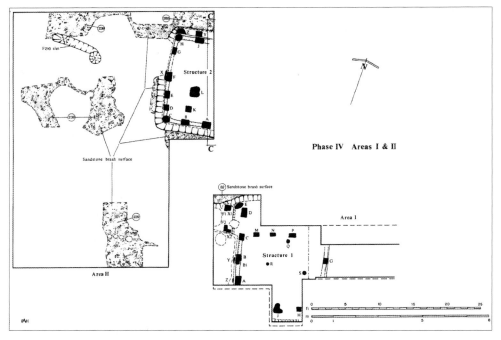

25 Lower Bridge Street (west) 1974-6. Plan of tenth-century buildings 1 and 2 as excavated.
© *Chester City Council*

Although modest in size, these buildings were robustly constructed. The wall-posts, judging from the dimensions of the locating-holes, were upwards of 300mm in diameter and were clearly intended to rise above ground level to support the walls and roof of a chamber over the cellar. There may even have been a further storey, or perhaps a loft space, above that again. Access to the cellar was gained externally by means of a flight of wooden steps set in a sloping passageway. A pair of small locating-holes found cut into the rock at the lower end of the passageway marked the position of the uprights for a door-frame. To prevent rainwater flooding the basement, this would have been covered by a simple porch projecting from the main body of the building. The walls of the buildings were probably formed of horizontal planking externally with perhaps an inner lining of more planks or possibly wattle and daub panels. The roof covering would have been either straw thatch laid on wattle hurdles or wooden shingles. The rubble produced by the excavation of the cellars was broken up and spread over the area around the buildings to form a solid surfacing. In one case, it was found that extra material had been laid down to form a ramped approach to the middle of the longer side of a building. It seems likely that this was the usual location for the main entrance into buildings of this type. It also suggests

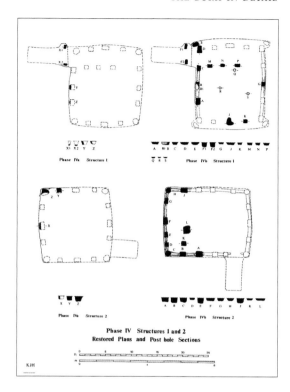

26 Lower Bridge Street (west) 1974-6.
Restored plans of tenth-century buildings
1 and 2. © *Chester City Council*

that the floor was elevated above the surrounding ground level by at least 0.20m, a feature which would have increased headroom in the basement and reduced the risk of damp rotting the floor.

All five of the buildings examined exhibited clear evidence of a second phase. The semi-sunken Building 4 had its wall posts renewed and a new clay floor laid down which sealed some of the original locating-holes around the perimeter of the floor area. A shallow slot found between certain of the post-settings probably held a grooved beam which acted as a base for the wall panels. In the cellared buildings the basement floor was lowered by the excavation of a further 30-40cm of rock followed by the creation of a new arrangement of post locating-holes. The sandstone rubble produced was used to re-surface the surrounding area. In Buildings 1 and 3 there was an additional line of locating-holes about 1m in from and running parallel to an end wall. In Building 1, but not in Building 2, this continued the alignment of the cellar entrance. The function of this extra line of posts, and the horizontal beam which they presumably supported, is unknown, but it may have been to carry the weight of some special feature at ground floor level, such as a hearth.

Building 1 differed from its neighbours in that it had not just one but two post-settings at the corners; a rectangular one in the usual position and another,

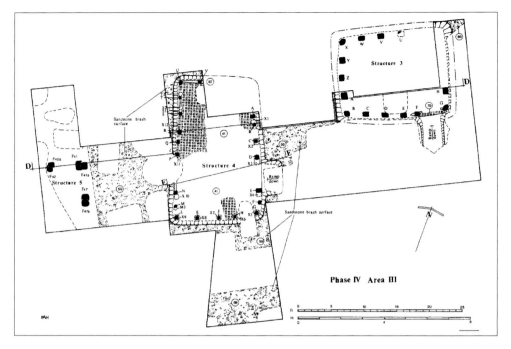

27 Lower Bridge Street (west) 1974-6. Plan of tenth-century buildings 3 and 4 as excavated.
© *Chester City Council*

oval in shape, immediately beyond it. In addition, along the ends of the building the pit dug to accommodate the cellar was made oversize leaving a gap of some 0.30m between the perimeter wall-posts and the neighbouring rock. It would seem that the gable ends of Building 1 received some form of special architectural treatment. There is no way of telling what form this took but the suggestion has been made that this was an early example of the use of a cruck-truss. In this form of construction, a pair of matched, curving timbers (obtained by cleaving or sawing down the middle of a carefully selected, naturally curving tree trunk) were placed together, in a configuration rather reminiscent of a wishbone, rising from the ground to meet at ridge level. Thus the main weight of the roof structure is borne by the crucks at the ends of the building, relieving the pressure on the walls. Crucks are often reinforced by horizontal beams linking the two 'legs' and preventing them from springing apart. The existence of such strengthening timbers might explain the gap between the rock face and the cellar walls at the ends of Building 1.

Cellared buildings like those excavated at Lower Bridge Street have been found in a number of other towns of this period in both England and Ireland and form a recognisable class of urban dwelling of the late Anglo-Saxon period.

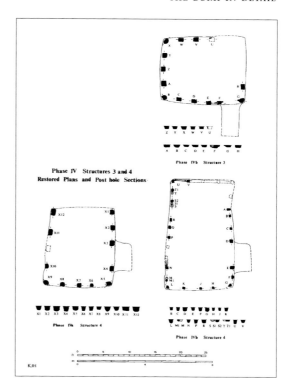

Phase IV Structures 3 and 4
Restored Plans and Post hole Sections

28 Lower Bridge Street (west) 1974-6.
Restored plans of tenth-century buildings
3 and 4. © *Chester City Council*

They are particularly common in areas of Scandinavian settlement or influence. The fact that both the end and the side walls of the Chester buildings exhibited a slight but distinct outwards curvature or bow is also to some degree a Scandinavian 'signature'. A design feature that reduced the risk of collapse during periods of high winds, it is a tradition reflected in the series of 'hog-backed' tombstones and house-shaped caskets from the northern and eastern parts of England, the areas where Scandinavian influence was greatest.[22] Common in the commercial quarters of many towns, these buildings can plausibly be interpreted as the dwellings of reasonably wealthy tradespeople. The cellars would have provided secure places of storage for the goods in which they traded as well as cool repositories for foodstuffs and other perishable materials. Little in the way of artefacts was recovered to indicate the nature of their use or the occupations of their inhabitants. A stone mould used in the production of metal ingots was retrieved from a layer associated with the abandonment of Building 4 (*30*).[23] The stone, a fragment of Horneblende-biotite-schist from the North West Highlands, is approximately 100mm long, rectangular in cross-section, and has 'reservoirs' cut into all four faces capable of producing small ingots of both U and V cross-section. The small size of the ingots implies that bars of precious rather than

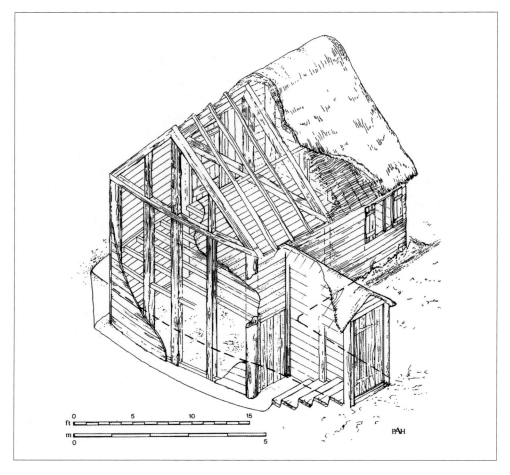

29 Lower Bridge Street (west) 1974-6. Reconstruction drawing of tenth-century buildings.
© *Chester City Council*

base metal were being produced, most likely silver ingots of the general type found in numerous Viking Age hoards, including the famous Castle Esplanade Hoard found at Chester in 1951 (see *40*) and a more modest example found near Heronbridge in 2001. Possibly one of the Lower Bridge Street buildings was inhabited by a jeweller or moneyer.

Dating evidence for the Lower Bridge Street buildings was scanty. Sherds of Chester ware pottery, introduced during the second quarter of the tenth century (see below), were completely absent from deposits contemporary with the original buildings and only a few were recovered from contexts associated with the end of their second phase. Given the solidity of their construction, both phases of the building could easily each have had a life of 20 years or more.

A date at some time in the period 900-925 for their initial appearance thus seems very plausible, while a planned scheme of development such as this would fit well into the context of the rejuvenation of the city's fortunes following the establishment of the *burh* in 907. Following the end of their second phase of use all of the above-mentioned buildings became derelict and the subterranean elements of the cellared or semi-cellared examples began to fill up with wind-blown and rain-washed material. After an interval of unknown duration, possibly a few years but probably not more than a decade or two, the former cellars took on a new lease of life in connection with the establishment of a leather-processing industry on the site (see below under 'Crafts & Industry'). On the spot where Building 4 had stood a new semi-sunken building was constructed. Unlike its predecessor the main wall-posts were founded in pits set back a short distance from the edge of the 0.90m deep interior giving the building overall dimensions of 6.06 x 3.94m. The south end of the floor area was occupied by a large clay and sandstone hearth which in all probability had an industrial function of some type.

The other buildings of Anglo-Saxon date found so far all lie inside the area of the old Roman fortress. Excavations at the east corner of the junction of modern Crook Street with Hamilton Place in 1971 encountered the remains of two phases of semi-sunken timber building, although they were only recognised as such when the site records were being worked up for publication.[24] Occupying an attractive corner site at the junction of Gerard's Lane with Crook Lane, the earlier and larger of the two buildings measured 7.15m in one dimension. Excavations further south and on the opposite side of Crook Street in 1973-4 disclosed the remains of more buildings (*31*). Initially considered to date to the late Roman period, detailed analysis for publication revealed them to belong to the Anglo-Scandinavian era.[25] Unlike most of the structures described so far, the buildings found on this site were ground-based. The remains consisted of two parallel rows of substantial post-pits set a little over 5m apart (like the Lower Bridge Street buildings, suggesting employment of the 'northern rod' of 5.03m). These lay parallel with Crook Street but ran at a slight angle to the alignment of the Roman barracks whose remains they cut. The post-settings, which averaged 0.30m in diameter and 0.50m in depth, are interpreted as the remains of two adjacent buildings set out one behind the other and facing east onto Gerard's Lane. Their location suggests that the still largely extant pattern of medieval property plots running back from Watergate Street originated well before the Conquest. Truncation of many of the deposits belonging to this period by later activity precluded the possibility of identifying floor levels while the lack of materials derived from the superstructure of these buildings suggests their fabric was composed entirely of perishable materials such as wood and straw.

30 Stone ingot mould.Lower Bridge Street (west) excavation 1974-6. © *Chester City Council*

Continuing northwards, investigations prior to the construction of the Princess Street/Hunter Street bus station in the late 1970s and early 1980s encountered substantial traces of tenth- and eleventh-century occupation (*32*). Excavation on the east side of Hunter's Walk exposed the successive surfacings of a north–south Roman street which ran down the west side of the enormous building lying behind the *principia*. The latest surfacing is thought to represent a late Anglo-Saxon restoration of this street as the foundations of a building of this period were cut directly through it without any interval which permitted the accumulation of soil or debris.[26] This putative street was traced northwards over a considerable distance and it may be that the entire length of this Roman thoroughfare was restored; in the opposite direction it was traced all the way to Goss Street. A medieval building found overlying the north-east corner of the baths attached to the Roman Elliptical Building occupied a position suggesting that Goss Street had once continued northwards beyond Hamilton Place and thus very probably as far as Princess Street.[27] At the southern end of the Hunter's Walk site it was found that the street had subsequently been built across when a timber building at least 12m long and a little over 5m wide (the northern rod again) was constructed. The building was raised on sizeable posts spaced 3m

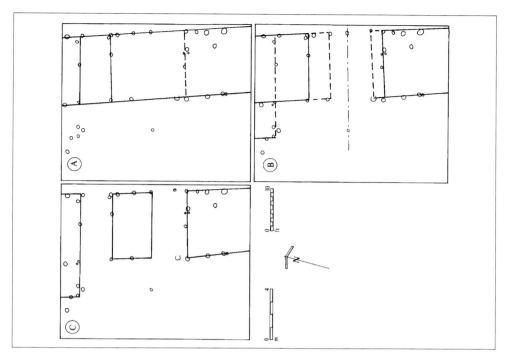

31 Crook Street excavation 1973-4. Plan of tenth-century buildings. © *Chester City Council*

apart. Traces of a small hearth were found inside the building and three spindle whorls were recovered from contemporary deposits immediately outside it. The impression gained is that this building's purpose was principally residential. The distribution of Chester ware pottery in contexts associated with this building suggests, like its construction across at least part of the roadway, that it belongs to the mid- or late tenth century.[28]

On the west side of the aforementioned street, excavation of the Hunter Street School site in 1979-81 disclosed that much of what had once been the walled compound of a Roman building had apparently been used for the penning of cattle and perhaps other animals in the mid-late Anglo-Saxon period. At some point in the tenth century this activity had ceased and the area was given over to market gardening or cultivation, a change which perhaps indicates an increasing urbanisation of the city centre.[29] At one spot within this general area the remains were found of the most humble form of structure belonging to this period. This was an example of a *Grubenhaus*, the German name for a small sunken-featured hut. The remains consisted of a sub-rectangular cut 0.34m deep and measuring 3.4m east–west by 2.5m north–south (*33*). The posts supporting the superstructure – consisting of lightweight walls sloping up to a central ridge-

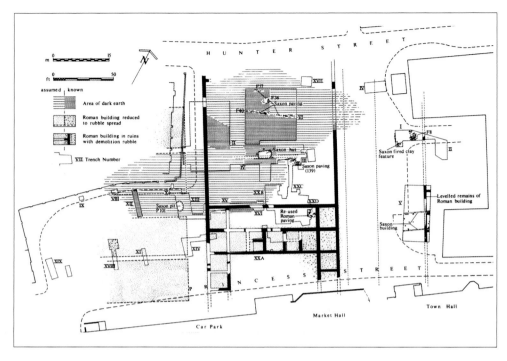

32 Princess Street area. Location of tenth-/eleventh-century structures. © *Chester City Council*

pole – were set in the ground a short distance back from the edge of the sunken area. The base (and sides) of the latter were lined with clay, which suggests it functioned as the actual floor rather than being covered over with planks resting on the pit edge like some examples.[30] If a dwelling, this structure would most probably have been occupied by a slave or slaves.

The final building to be mentioned is a conventional ground-based example found in the south-west portion of the area encompassed by the Abbey Green excavations of 1975-8. Located at the southern edge of the perimeter road, this covered a sizeable area measuring a minimum of 7 x 8m but its purpose and detailed plan could not be determined. It may have been a workshop associated with blacksmithing (*34*).[31]

On the evidence recovered so far, the creation of the *burh* in 907 paved the way for a rapid expansion in the physical development and prosperity of the city. There was certainly plenty of land available on which to construct dwellings and other buildings. Many of the lesser buildings of the Roman fortress, such as the barracks, had long since decayed and collapsed, becoming nettle-covered piles of rubble easily cleared when required. Much of the reusable building stone would presumably have been recycled as the fabric of the new churches and associated

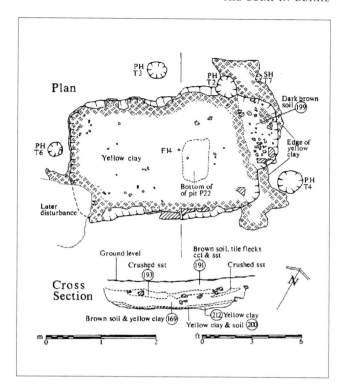

Plan

PH T3

PH T2

SH T7

Dark brown soil 199

PH T6

Yellow clay

F14

Edge of yellow clay

PH T4

Bottom of of pit P22

Later disturbance

Ground level

Brown soil, tile flecks ccl & sst 191

Crushed sst 193

Crushed sst

Cross Section

Brown soil & yellow clay 169

212 Yellow clay
Yellow clay & soil 200

N

m 0   1   2   ft 0   3   6

33 Hunter Street School excavation 1979 & 1981. Plan of tenth-century sunken-featured structure. © *Chester City Council*

ecclesiastical buildings erected during the tenth century. Even some of the larger Roman buildings had been cleared away by the end of the first millennium. As described above, the west range of the enormous complex behind the *principia* was built across at this time while what remained of its eastern range was probably demolished to allow the construction of Northgate Street. The uncovering of part of the cross-hall of the *principia* itself in 1897 revealed the remains of its columns lying where they had fallen when the building collapsed.[32] Some of these can still be seen and it is evident from their position relative to the bases on which they once stood that less than 20cm of earth or debris had accumulated over the *principia* floor by the time they fell. This in turn implies that the cross-hall at least did not survive many centuries into the post-Roman period. At the southern end of the *principia*, excavations a short distance west of the present St Peter's in 1985 found evidence for the systematic clearance of its remains and the levelling of its site in the post-Roman period. The lack of artefacts associated with this event makes it difficult to date but it would fit well with the general reorganisation of the fortress interior following the creation of the *burh*. It also occurred soon after a brief spate of activity on the site represented by the digging of pits for the burial of material which the excavator suggested might derive from the soiled floor-coverings of temporary buildings.[33] The sort of occupation this suggests is similar to that encountered on the Lower Bridge Site and dated to the later ninth century.

Because of their sheer massiveness and solidity there are a few buildings which most probably survived as imposing ruins for some time, continuing largely unaffected by the evolving townscape around them. Chief among these would be the bathing complexes with their stone-faced concrete walls over a metre thick rising, in the major examples, to over 15m in height. As described in chapter 2, parts of the main fortress baths survived intact for a considerable period after AD 400; long enough for a 40cm-thick layer of earth, possibly derived at least in part from occupation of the building, to accumulate on the floor of the main bathing-halls before the vaulted concrete roof finally collapsed (*colour plate 1*).[34] Elements of this vast complex were sufficiently robust structurally that they could have been used and occupied for many centuries. Unfortunately it is impossible to prove that this actually happened, as the conditions under which all major explorations have occurred so far were not conducive to the investigation of this particular aspect of the baths' history. What is clear, however, is that extensive portions of Roman masonry must have been standing to a height of at least several metres above ground level over large areas of the area east of the Bridge Street frontage for several hundred years after the *burh*'s foundation. Elements of the substantially constructed Elliptical Building and its adjacent baths are also likely to have survived above ground level into the Norman period.

Outside the fortress, two buildings come to mind as likely candidates for survival as substantial ruins. The first is the principal extramural bathing complex situated on the north side of the road which in the early Roman period serviced the harbour and which is now perpetuated by Lower Watergate Street. This covered an area at least 90m square and from the quality of the remains seen in the late eighteenth century probably remained undisturbed until the construction of the Francisan friary in the early thirteenth century. The other building is of course the amphitheatre. Assuming that neighbouring St John's was founded *c*.689 then pillaging of stone from the amphitheatre's fabric probably began at quite an early date and continued in periodic bursts of intense activity as and when the church buildings were expanded and/or increased. There is some evidence, for example, that the outer wall of the amphitheatre on the south side had already been largely demolished down to ground level by the end of the tenth century.[35] It is equally clear, however, that the amphitheatre site continued to be a recognisable feature of the landscape for many centuries. Indeed, it was only in the early part of the eighteenth century that the hollow marking the position of the arena was finally filled in. Possibly the amphitheatre had martyrial connotations – either real or imagined – for the early Church in

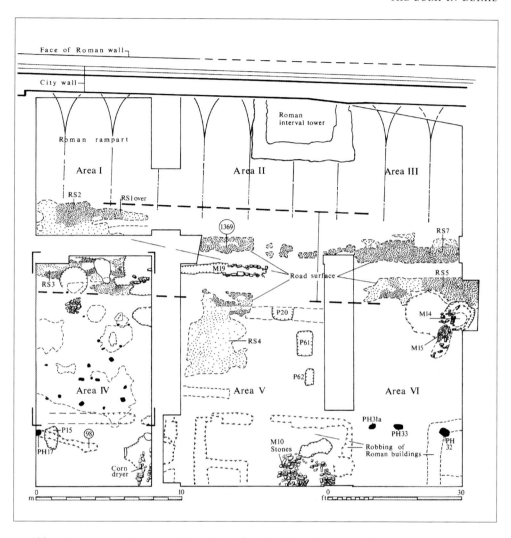

Face of Roman wall

City wall

Roman rampart

Roman interval tower

Area I

Area II

Area III

RS2

RS1 over

1369

RS7

RS3

M19

Road surface

RS5

P20

M14

RS4

P61

M15

P62

Area IV

Area V

Area VI

PH31a

PH33

P15

98

M10 Stones

Robbing of Roman buildings

PH 32

PH17

Corn dryer

0   m   10   0   ft   30

34 Abbey Green excavation 1975-8. Location of tenth-/eleventh-century features.
© *Chester City Council*

Chester. It could also have been used for secular celebrations associated with Church festivals or ceremonies including perhaps those which undoubtedly accompanied King Edgar's symbolic coronation at St John's in 973.

Thus, it can be said in summary that occupation in tenth-century Chester covered a wide area, both within the former legionary fortress and immediately beyond it. However, in many areas the buildings were quite dispersed with extensive patches of open ground between them either lying completely derelict or used as the setting for industrial or horticultural activity.

MATERIAL CULTURE

The stimulus both to trade and to the mass production of goods which the Scandinavian settlement provided means that the period after c.900 is represented by a number and range of artefacts far greater than that available for earlier periods. Among the more common finds are items associated with clothing and personal adornment. Hooked tags are one such, made usually of bronze but occasionally of silver or lead alloy. Found on many urban sites including Dublin, Lincoln, Winchester and York, they were used as an all-purpose clothes fastener in much the same way as 'hooks and eyes'.[36] Those found in Chester have plates generally either circular or triangular in shape. They have been found both inside and outside the area of the former Roman fortress and some examples can be paralleled by examples from Meols at the tip of the Wirral. The variations in form have given rise to the suggestion that they were imported into Chester from a number of workshops throughout the country.[37]

The bronze ring-headed pins common in Ireland were quickly adopted by the Vikings for fastening cloaks, being worn either on the right shoulder or centrally. Such pins were held in place by a length of cord tied to the ring and then to the shaft after it had passed through the cloth. At least half a dozen examples are known from Chester and all are of copper alloy apart from the ring of one made of silver found during the Northgate Brewery excavation of 1974-5. The pins varied between 10 and 15cm in length. Some have a flattened area towards the tip decorated with a narrow panel of interlace ornament. The head is usually cubic in shape, sometimes with facetted corners, and two opposing sides are either deeply grooved or pierced right through to accommodate the freely swivelling penannular ring. The head can be plain, engraved in part, or decorated with punched dots and incised lines. The rings are either circular or square in cross-section and in some cases bear further decoration.

Pins without a ring at the head were also used and a fine example was recovered during rescue excavation of the legionary baths in 1963-4, though unfortunately from an unstratified context. Just under 10cm long, this has a spherical head decorated with a raised triskele motif. Below the head are two slight collars and below these again, set diametrically opposite one another, are a cross and a rune executed in what appears to be silver inlay (35). Both the triskele design and the cross can be paralleled on Irish examples. The rune ᚴ or 'k' – perhaps an abbreviation for 'Christ' – has a distribution restricted to north-west England.[38] The rune is the first example in this script to be found in Chester and only the second from the whole of Cheshire, the other being the Athelmund memorial found at Overchurch on the Wirral.

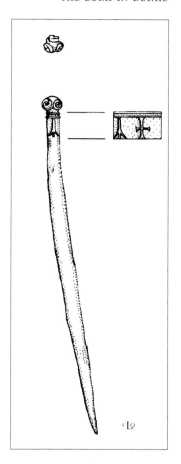

35 Legionary Baths excavation 1963-4. Tenth-/eleventh-century copper alloy round-headed pin with raised triskele pattern decoration with opposed cross and rune below.
© *Chester City Council*

Brooches of this period are rare finds in Chester but the two recovered so far are particularly fine examples. The less well preserved but more valuable piece – made of the purest silver – comes from the Lower Bridge excavations of 1974-6 (*colour plate 20*). Although found in a medieval rubbish-pit its form and decoration place it firmly in the second half of the ninth century and it had presumably been disturbed from its original context by the digging of the pit. Given its value and the degree of wear visible on its surface it may well have been in circulation for some considerable time before being lost or discarded. Thus its original owner could have been living in Chester either just before or just after the foundation of the *burh*. Like most brooches of the period it is circular in shape, measuring 3.7cm in diameter. The overall pattern takes the form of an expanded-arm cross, with volute-shaped terminals, created by carefully executed cut-outs in the metal. Tiny blue glass inlays, of which only two survive, were originally enclosed in the volutes. In the centre of the cross is a boss which was also the head of a rivet. There were two further smaller rivets located in the middle of the terminals of two opposing arms. These would have held in place a unit consisting of back strip, catch-plate and hinged pin. The voluted terminals of the arms of the cross touch and produce in the void between the arms a pear-shaped feature giving the appearance of a three-lobed leaf. Within a plain border there is a pattern of delicate interlace design which originally covered the body of the cross but which is now much corroded.[39]

The second brooch was found near the centre of the Roman fortress during the investigation of the Hunter Street School site in 1981.[40] It, too, is a disc brooch but this one is made of copper alloy, cast in two pieces, and is slightly smaller at 3.2cm in diameter (36 and cover illustration). The two discs are held together by a central rivet and the undecorated lower one bears two pin-attachment lugs along with a catch plate and a small attachment loop. The upper convex disc is decorated with openwork, zoomorphic ornament consisting of a single interlacing animal within a grooved border. The animal head is shown in profile facing right and has a large round eye. Its back is linked with its beak-like jaws by an oval loop, interlacing with the neck and body. The ribbon-shaped body is defined by double lines and the elongated neck extends across the field to the forequarters (on the right). The body continues to form an arc below the head to the hindquarters (on the left). The foreleg crosses over the neck and the hind leg behind while its claw-like footrests on the upper part of the foreleg. The grooved tail forms a loop around the upper part of the hind leg. The decorative treatment belongs to the Jellinge style of Viking art fashionable for much of the tenth century. Four other similar brooches are known from the British Isles, the closest in detail being one found in Dublin.[41] Other examples have been found in both Denmark and Sweden and, very recently, Iceland.[42]

In addition to metalwork there is a modest assemblage of decorated bone objects to illustrate aspects of everyday life in Viking Age Chester. Two examples of thin, tongue-shaped plaques used as belt- or strap-ends have come to light, one from the Abbey Green investigations of 1975-8 and the other during rescue excavation on the site of the south-west angle-tower of the legionary fortress in 1964. The example found at Abbey Green is the larger of the pair at 9cm in length by 1.6cm wide. It is decorated on one side only with a simple interlace pattern (37).

Unlike the other example, it is missing the recessed and pierced section at the inner square end where the strap was attached by rivets. The piece from the south-west angle-tower is carved on one side only with a tree-like pattern in the upper part of which two birds stand facing outwards but with their heads turned to meet one another over a central flower or spur of foliage (38). This design, known as the 'Tree of Life,' has a very ancient lineage. The tree is one of the

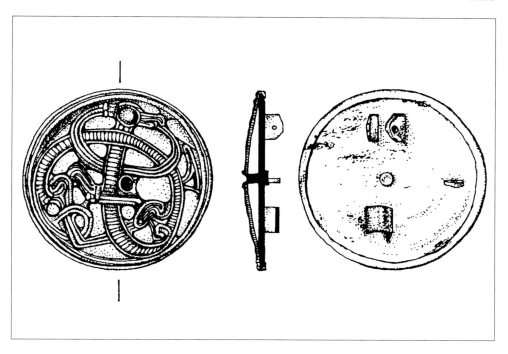

36 Copper alloy brooch with Jellinge style decoration. Hunter Street School excavation 1979 & 1981.
© *Chester City Council*

oldest traditional symbols, representing the life of the cosmos through its ability to grow, proliferate and regenerate, and its longevity compared to man's short lifespan. In Christian iconography it could be seen as a symbolic linking together of heaven, earth and the underworld through its leaves, trunk and roots, or as a metaphor for the cross of Redemption upon which the Saviour of Mankind died. Similarly, for the non-Christian the tree could be equated with the world-tree Yggdrasil of north European mythology. The symbol occurs quite commonly in the ninth and tenth centuries on a variety of objects from northern Europe, including jewellery, buckles and strap-ends such as this, and in metal as well as bone.[43]

Combs and comb cases form a second group of bone objects. A fragment of a particulary fine example was found during rescue recording of the fortress baths in 1963-4. This comes from a double-sided comb made of two panels joined by iron rivets (thus known as the composite type). It is decorated with widely spaced double lines of cross-hatching arranged to form a lattice pattern (*39*). The side plate for a comb case was found during excavations at 17-19 Watergate street in 1985. Carved from antler, this was decorated with groups of three or four incisions spaced widely apart.[44]

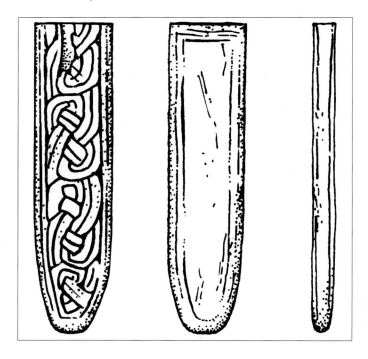

37 Tenth-century bone plaque with incised interlace decoration. Abbey Green excavation 1975-8. © *Chester City Council*

Iron objects would certainly have been used and manufactured in Anglo-Scandinavian Chester but the ironwork found in deposits of this period is usually so fragmented and corroded that it is difficult to distinguish individual items from their Roman counterparts, which survive in considerable numbers as residual material within the fortress area. A notable exception is the high-quality, pattern-welded blade belonging to a *seax* or long-knife found during the 1975-8 Abbey Green excavation. Such knives were used as weapons, not domestic implements, and it is thought that the name 'Saxons' was derived from this, their most common weapon. The large, single-edged blade has a kicked-back and straight edge, the back dropping to meet the blade at a long, sharply pointed tip. The short, rectangular tang bears minerally preserved organic remains of its hazel wood handle.[45]

The first half of the tenth century witnessed the re-birth of the pottery industry in many parts of England, with large numbers of vessels produced in significant quantities for the first time since the Roman period. At Chester, the initial identification of pottery of this period was made possible by the discovery in 1950 of the Castle Esplanade coin-hoard, deposited *c.*970, because the container used was a pottery jar (*40*). Once the characteristics of the pottery – understandably given the name 'Chester ware' – were known it opened the way for its recognition on many subsequent excavations throughout the city. However, the sherds were usually found occurring residually amongst the material recovered from later

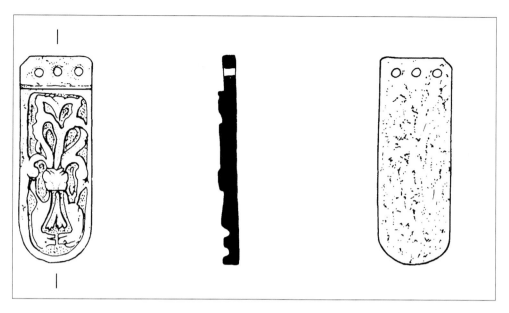

38 Tenth-/eleventh-century bone plaque with 'Tree-of-Life' decoration found during south-west angle tower excavation of 1964-5. © *Chester City Council*

deposits and it was not until the Lower Bridge Street excavation of 1974-6 that a wide range of the earliest types of this pottery were retrieved from a contemporary stratigraphic sequence.[46] Subsequently, significant collections of this pottery were recovered from excavations inside the old fortress area, the largest coming from the Abbey Green Site investigated 1975-8.[47] Excavations at many other urban centres in the Midlands and the West around the same time yielded similar pottery, sometimes in even greater quantities and in a few cases in association with the remains of the kilns where it was manufactured. To have continued calling the pottery 'Chester ware' would obviously have been somewhat misleading as well as factually inaccurate, so instead the term 'Chester-type Wares' was introduced. However, it was definitely the variant produced at Chester that was exported to Dublin in significant quantities.[48] A precise date for the beginning of such pottery at Chester has yet to be obtained. It occurs at Dublin in contexts which also produce coins of Athelstan (924-39) and at Hereford in deposits dated to the second quarter of the tenth century.[49] It seems very likely, therefore, that large-scale pottery production commenced some time around 910-20 in response to the increase in trade stimulated both by the beginnings of urbanisation and Scandinavian settlement and spread rapidly thereafter. The production of Chester-type wares appears to have ceased around the middle of the eleventh century for reasons as yet unknown.

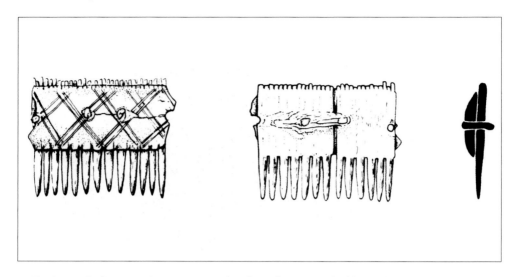

39 Legionary Baths excavation 1963-4. Tenth-/eleventh-century double-sided composite bone comb. © *Chester City Council*

40 Chester-ware pot used as container for Castle Esplanade hoard. © *Chester City Council*

41 Rubbings of impressed band decoration on examples of Chester-ware pottery. © *Chester City Council*

42 Fragment of tenth-century sculpture from St John's church

Chester ware pottery usually has a hard and sandy texture and contains rounded quartz grits up to 1mm in diameter. The surface varies from light-orange or yellowish through reddish-brown, while the core is generally grey. The regularity of the rims and other features suggest the vessels were trued-up on a wheel if not actually wheel-thrown. Jars and bowls were the two main classes of vessel produced, although an example of a spouted pitcher was found on the Abbey Green Site.[50] The rim forms are generally quite simple with a degree of development over time and some of the jars appear designed to have had lids. Decoration is common, usually consisting of a single band of impressed lattice pattern on the shoulder of the jars and just below the rim on bowls. Occasionally, this also occurs on the rim itself (*41*). A few examples of complete or only slightly damaged jars have been found, such as the Castle Esplanade Hoard pot, an example found near the Queen's Head Hotel, Foregate Street, in 1938 and one discovered during the Hunter Street School excavations of 1979–81 (*colour plate 27*).

Sculpture belonging to this period is represented solely by examples of the flourishing stone-mason's workshop operating near St John's (*42*). The heads of six ring-headed crosses with bossed spandrels were recovered from the churchyard and from the rubble of the collapsed west tower in 1870.[51] Other crosses thought to have originated from the same workshop have been found at various sites both on the Wirral and in neighbouring Flintshire.[52]

CHURCHES

Three of Chester's churches were definitely pre-Conquest foundations: St Werburgh (originally perhaps SS Peter & Paul), St John the Baptist and St Peter. If the medieval chroniclers are to be believed, the first of these was already of 'high antiquity' when St Werburgh's remains were transferred here in 875 from Hanbury.[53] When Chester was restored in 907, Aethelflaed rebuilt this church, re-dedicated it to St Werburgh and transferred the old dedication to a new church – St Peter's – located opposite the junction of the old *via praetoria* and *via principalis*. The image of a church shown on Edward's 'minster' penny might be a representation of the new church of St Werburgh, apparently equipped with a western tower and either aisles or side chapels. Further endowments by Aethelstan enabled the institution of a college of secular canons and the foundation prospered. A charter of Edgar's lists yet more benefactions, including a series of manors recorded in the Domesday Survey which enjoyed the highly unusual privilege of exemption from maintenance of the *burh* defences and the bridge over the Dee. Earl Leofric was a major patron in the eleventh century and by 1066 St Werburgh's was the richest landowner in the county apart from the Earl himself. Sadly, we have no archaeological information about the pre-Conquest church and its attendant buildings, but we do know from Domesday that the warden and canons occupied thirteen houses in the city free of dues.[54]

St John's was reputedly founded in 689 and was certainly already a sizeable establishment by the mid-tenth century when it was the scene of a ceremony celebrating Edgar's coronation.[55] Its situation just outside the *burh* defences in the suburb of Redcliff – so called because of the adjacent sandstone river-cliff – might indicate that it was founded after SS Peter & Paul, with the latter already having rights over most of the area of the old fortress interior. There could easily have been other reasons, however, including the possibility of a martyrial cult associated with Christians who had been executed in the adjacent amphitheatre in the third century. There was also a monastery of St Mary near Redcliff, mentioned in Domesday but otherwise unattested. St John's, like St Werburgh's, was a substantial collegiate institution with extensive parishes.[56] Domesday records eight houses belonging to St John's located '*in civitate*' ('in the city' – and thus inside the defended area) and these are most likely to have been situated along Newgate Street. For a brief period after the Conquest St John's became the principal church of the Lichfield diocese. In 1075 Bishop Peter formally moved his see to Chester, but within a decade or two it was transferred to Coventry.[57] A burial found close to the southern outer wall of the amphitheatre in 2001 has been dated to the tenth century. Situated about 100m west of St John's (assuming the pre-Conquest church stood on more or less the same site as its successor), this perhaps gives an indication of the size to which the cemetery around it had grown by this period (source needed).[58] A collection of sculpture (described above) is the only other material evidence of the tenth-century St John's.

Again according to the medieval chroniclers, St Peter's was founded when the *burh* was established in 907 by Aethelflaed. Along with St Werburgh's and St John's, there have been no opportunities for archaeological investigation, so tangible evidence of their size, plan and structural development is lacking.

On the basis of their Hiberno-Norse dedications, St Bridget's and St Olaf's (now St Olave's) were also probably pre-Conquest foundations. The former stood immediately outside and to the west of the south gate of the Roman fortress. It was demolished when Grosvenor Street was built in the early nineteenth century and replaced by a new church of the same name (itself demolished in the 1960s) at a location close to what is now the Grosvenor roundabout. St Olaf's still stands, on the south side of the junction of St Olave's Lane with Lower Bridge Street. The sandstone masonry of this modest church is obviously of considerable antiquity (apart from sections restored after a severe fire in the twentieth century) but whether it dates back as far as the eleventh century is a moot point (King Olaf died in 1030).

THE CHESTER MINT

It was Offa who introduced the first standardised coin to be used in Britain since the Roman period. This was the silver penny, and was produced by moneyers working under licence in the principal settlements of the realm. These gradually increased in number as the network of *burhs* begun by Alfred was extended over a wider area and the degree of economic activity increased. The modern connotation of the denomination 'penny' implies a coin of the low value but in fact the Anglo-Saxon penny was of considerable worth – more akin to the gold sovereign – and it was not intended for small transactions. Where such coins of ninth and tenth century date are found in large numbers it implies the settlement concerned was a major centre of commercial activity. The moneyers who, as far as we know, worked on an individual basis, not in any single mint building, struck coins from dies issued by the king. The dies were distributed from a small number of centres, perhaps including Chester, at intervals of six or sometimes three years. The moneyers had to pay a substantial fee for the dies, which at Chester in the time of Edward the Confessor was 13 shillings and 4 pence to the king and 6 shillings and 8 pence to the earl. It was the duty of the moneyers to guarantee personally the weight and precious metal content of the coinage. So that any moneyer trying to take more than their allotted share as commission by adding baser metals could easily be identified, their name had to appear on the coins. Severe penalties – usually the removal of a hand – awaited any moneyer found guilty of committing fraud. The requirement for moneyers to put their names on their coins, as well as the location of the mint, makes them a useful source of information about the ethnic origins of the population in particular settlements and this aspect of the Chester mint is discussed below.

In addition to newly mined silver, much of the raw material used by the moneyers consisted of foreign and obsolete coins which were not regarded as legal tender, along with the chopped-up bullion or 'hacksilber' favoured by Viking traders, which could include fragments of jewellery and vessels as well as small ingots (see *40*). Collections of such material buried as hoards by their owners for safekeeping either while they were away or in times of danger and never recovered constitute an important source of information about coins and silver in this period. Chester has produced a number of hoards, the most famous of which (not least because of the story surrounding its discovery) is probably the Castle Esplanade hoard found in 1950 at a spot on the west side of Nicholas Street opposite what is now the Magistrates' Court. It was found by workmen digging a trench to lay an electricity cable and unfortunately was not reported at the time. Some of the workmen put handfuls of coins in their pockets; others were given to children; and the rest shovelled back into the trench.[59]

43 Coin minted at Chester 915-20
with image of stone tower, perhaps
representing the restored defences.
© *British Museum*

A few months later news of the discovery reached the ears of the Curator of
the Grosvenor Museum – then Graham Webster – who set about recovering as
much of the material as he could and also mounted his own excavation at the
site of the discovery. As a result of his magnificent efforts the bulk of the hoard
was recovered. It was declared Treasure Trove at the subsequent coroner's inquest,
and thus saved for the nation. The workmen who returned material received a
financial reward. In addition, Graham Webster himself was awarded £400 – not
far short of a year's salary at the time – but he waived his claim in order to
secure 300 of the coins not required by the British Museum for the Grosvenor
Museum, along with all of the bullion. Further coins and other material were
handed in years later by others involved in the original discovery or their
relatives. The hoard had originally been buried around 970 in a cooking-pot
and consisted of about 500 pennies from all over England (though chiefly from
the Chester mint), along with hacksilber sufficient to mint about another 750
pennies and comprising brooch fragments, pieces of bracelets, lengths of wire, as
well as 98 ingots both complete and in part. The largest ingots averaged 117mm
in length and 15mm in width with an average weight of 128g. A stone mould
for casting ingots was found during excavation of the Lower Bridge Street site
in 1974, an indication perhaps that one of the substantial cellared buildings
there was occupied by a moneyer (see *30*). Certain items of metalwork in the
hoard have led to the suggestion that it was the property of a Norse merchant
or moneyer who had connections with the Isle of Man and perhaps the
Hebrides.[60]

44 Coin minted at Chester 915-20 bearing image of a tower or, perhaps more likely, a reliquary, possibly containing the remains of St Werburgh. © *British Museum*

The coins in the Castle Esplanade hoard range in date from the reign of Alfred to that of Edgar, and it may have been a savings hoard rather than material about to be melted down by a moneyer. Another hoard also deposited *c.*970, found on the north side of Eastgate Street in 1857, is probably more representative of the coinage in current circulation. Almost 90% of the coins belong to the reign of Edgar, indicating that the collection was amassed over a short period of time immediately before it was buried. Just over 80% of the coins in this hoard were minted at Chester. Yet a third hoard, deposited around 980, was found just within the line of the city walls, near the partially rebuilt tower known as Pemberton's Parlour. The final hoard found at Chester was discovered near St John's Church in 1862. This was deposited around 924 and may have been buried during the turmoil associated with the revolt of the city against Edward the Elder.

The precise date at which the Chester mint first commenced operations is not known. The *burh* name first appears on coins during the reign of Athelstan (924-39), but numismatists have been able to show from a study of types and styles that coins were being minted at Chester considerably earlier and quite possibly from *c.*890.[61] During the reign of Athelstan the Chester mint produced more coins than any other in the whole of England. There were more than twenty moneyers working in the city, compared with fewer than ten in London and

45 Example of the so-called Minster type of coin minted at Chester 915-20 bearing an image of one of the new churches in the city, either St Werburgh's or St Peter's. © *British Museum*

only seven at Winchester. The refounding of Chester as a *burh* by Aethelflaed was undoubtedly instrumental in the upsurge in economic activity, for it allowed the city to exploit its location at the intersection of land and sea trade-routes.

The output of the mint would also have been boosted by processing the spoils of war such as the silver taken from the Danes in 916-18, the looting of York in 928 and the booty captured at the battle of *Brunanburh* in 937. It is noteworthy that the Chester mint-mark is the most common on English coins found in tenth-century Irish hoards.[62] The distribution of hoards in Ireland containing Chester coins suggests that Dublin was the main port of entry and this is borne out by the high incidence of coins bearing the Chester mint-mark found in excavations in Dublin itself.[63] Hoards from all around the Irish Sea attest the predominance of the Chester mint in the region. A considerable number of coins bearing the Chester mint-mark also occur in hoards throughout Scandinavia.[64]

As mentioned in chapter five, the coinage produced by the Chester mint included an unusual group of pictorial types issued in the period *c*.915-924. One, the so-called 'Minster' type, depicts a church − presumably either the new St Peter's or the rebuilt church of SS Peter & Paul, now dedicated to St Werburgh (*45*). Another shows a stone tower, taken to be a representation of some upstanding part of the Roman defences (*43*). A third type, once also regarded as a depiction of a tower, is now thought to show a reliquary (*44*).[65]

CRAFTS AND INDUSTRY

Many of the industries which must have been carried out in Chester are represented by their products or in a few cases their raw materials, rather than by the remains of the structures where they were actually made. Thus, while we have metalwork, pottery, bonework and coins, we have relatively little information as to in which part or parts of the city their manufacture was located. Given that both the scale and means of production was in most cases quite modest and the opportunities for locating the physical remains in an urban environment are so limited this is hardly surprising. There were plenty of large open areas in tenth- and eleventh-century Chester where kilns, furnaces and similar structures could have been accommodated, while the fact that industries were generally carried out by individuals means that they could be very dispersed rather than concentrated in one area. Some activities were so specialised that they leave little physical traces. For example, we are unlikely to find much evidence of the activities of moneyers and workers of precious metals beyond the occasional discovery of a hoard of coins and bullion or the odd lucky find such as the ingot mould recovered on the Lower Bridge Street site.

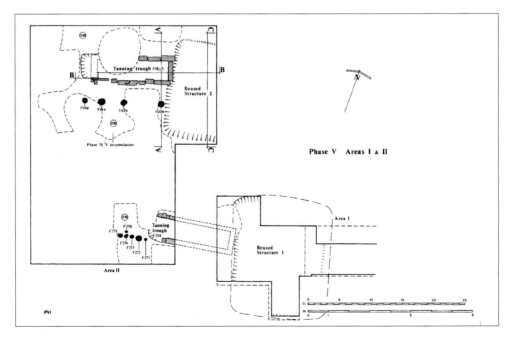

46 Lower Bridge Street (west) excavation 1974-6. Plan of eleventh-century tanning industry features. © Chester City Council

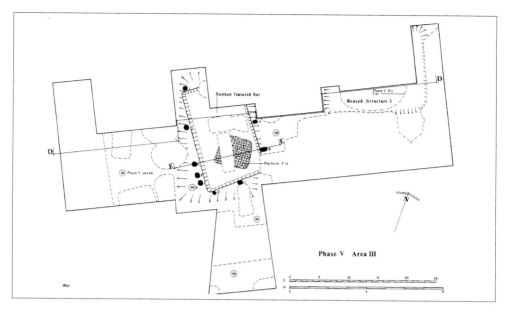

47 Lower Bridge Street (west) excavation 1974-6. Plan of eleventh-century building. © *Chester City Council*

Excavations over the last 30 years have provided two exceptions to the above general rule. The first concerns the 1974-6 investigations west of Lower Bridge Street. It was described previously how the tenth-century buildings belonging to a planned scheme of development became derelict at the end of the second phase of usage.[66] The period of abandonment was sufficient to allow the former cellars of the buildings to become partly filled with naturally deposited material. This process was terminated by a phase of new activity on the site which saw the former cellars largely cleaned out ready for re-use. The nature of their new role was clear from the fill that subsequently accumulated in them, which consisted of numerous layers of dark greasy silt containing minute fragments of leather. The impression that this was the residue from hide-processing and tanning operations was confirmed by the contemporary structures erected in association with the former cellars (46).

At both of the two northernmost examples a rectangular, stone-lined trough was constructed at right-angles to their west side. A little over 4m long, and about 1m wide and 1.20m deep, these ran right up to the edge of the former cellar. The northern, and more extensively explored, example had had a roofed timber structure erected over it supported by posts set back 1m from the trough sides (47). Its neighbour, by contrast, had a similar if narrower timber structure beyond its western terminus. These constructions were obviously where the hides were soaked and the unwanted materials such as hair and fat scraped off. The troughs may also have been used for actually tanning the leather by soaking in water containing quantities of wood or bark. It would seem that the unwanted residues which collected in the base of the trough were periodically shovelled or flushed out into the neighbouring 'cellar'. Similar residues were found in the cellar of the Building 3 located some distance to the south while a new building of this period was erected partially overlying Building 4 of the original scheme (*47*).

The leather industry in the Lower Bridge Street area was obviously quite significant in scale and it would seem that this was where the beginnings lay of what was to become the most important industry of medieval Chester. Guilds of tanners, wet and dry glovers, cordwainers and shoemakers, skinners and feltmakers and saddlers and curriers are all recorded in medieval Chester.[67] The skinners and glovers mainly operated along the stretch of riverbank running west from the Old Dee Bridge to the area of the Little Roodee, known as the Gloverhouses or Skinnerhouses, and continued to do so until the late eighteenth century. Possibly these crafts migrated or were forced to move closer to the river as areas like the frontages of Lower Bridge Street were laid out as burgage plots in the twelfth century. The glovers' activities also gave rise to the curious place-name Gloverstone – 'the glover's stone' – which was applied to a polygonal-shaped area of land east and south-east of the castle. The name derived from a large blue-grey stone which stood outside the castle gate until the late nineteenth century. It was one of a number in the city and its environs apparently used to define manorial and other administrative boundaries, which also seem to have been used as convenient objects by glovers for dressing leather.[68] Further east along the riverbank, Souter's Lane, running from the river up to the Newgate, takes its name from the shoemakers who worked in the area.

The Abbey Green excavations of 1975-8 at the north end of the city produced evidence for no fewer than three separate industrial activities, albeit all on a small scale. Grain processing was represented by the remains of a corn-drying kiln, consisting of a stone-lined flue channel several metres long and about 0.35m deep and wide (see *34* & *colour plate 24*). The stoking-pit at the outer end of the flue was also excavated but the base of the main body of the kiln lay beyond the excavated area. The structure's function was clear from the deposits of charcoal and grain in the flue channel and its size suggests that substantial quantities of grain were dried in one go before being taken away for threshing and milling.[69] The remains of a timber building were found a short distance to the north of the corn-drying kiln. Its plan could not be recovered but it seems likely to have had an industrial function given that a group of hearths were found immediately to its north. Their remains consisted of four shallow, circular depressions varying from 1-2m in diameter; two lined with clay and the other two with a base formed of rubble. Substantial quantities of iron-smithing slag were recovered from neighbouring deposits. Layers of charcoal and some signs of burning were evident but not of the type one would expect from the high temperatures achieved in metal-working hearths. Nonetheless, the evidence taken as a whole suggest that one or more blacksmiths were operating on the site. The third industrial activity was represented by features situated some 25m to the east of the timber building. These consisted of a pit – stone-lined in its later phases of use, a clay and stone sluice-like structure, and a rubble-filled hollow (see *34* and *colour plate 25*). A substantial quantity of sawn antler fragments was found both in and around these features as well as in the deposits which filled them suggesting that they were the focus of an antler-working industry. Soaking antler made it easier to cut and carve. The antler was perhaps immersed in the pit for a period and then removed to be washed in the neighbouring hollow which, with its rubble base, would have functioned as a soak-away.

As to the dating of these industrial activities, Chester ware pottery occurred freely throughout the associated contexts indicating usage in the later tenth century or the eleventh century. The corn-drying kiln, however, appeared to the report writer to be earlier than the other features, perhaps belonging to the period before the construction of the defensive perimeter road when part of the Abbey Green area was cultivated.[70] If so, then it might be contemporary with the later phases of agricultural activity on the Lower Bridge Street site, both brought to an end perhaps by the creation of the *burh*. The area which included the Abbey Green site is recorded as having been granted to St Werburgh's at the time of its re-foundation as an abbey in 1093 by Hugh Lupus, the first Earl of Chester (indeed, much of it is still held by its successor, the Dean and Chapter of Chester Cathedral). Thus, the widespread if non-intensive activity found by the 1970s excavation should be viewed in connection with properties along the Northgate Street frontage rather than workshops serving the earlier college of secular canons of St Werburgh. This interpretation is supported by the very considerable quantity of pottery recovered from the site, which suggests residential occupation nearby, not the distant St Werburgh's.

THE PORT AND TRADE

Chester's geographical location and the natural assets it possessed played a crucial role in its early medieval development, just as they had when the Romans chose the site hundreds of years earlier. The history and development of the kingdoms around it meant that by the beginning of the tenth century the city stood astride a major ethnic, political and military fault-line with English Mercia to the south and south-east, the Welsh kingdoms to the west, the Danelaw to the east and north-east, and the Norse Vikings across the Irish sea. The centre of military conflict in times of war, a frontier location such as this in peacetime was the focus of substantial trade, a situation reinforced by the site's nodal position on natural communication routes. It was on the direct route between North Wales and North-West England, while to the south and south-east the old Roman road system connected the region with Mercia and, ultimately, London. The Dee estuary provided access to the sea routes connecting the wealthy trading settlements scattered around the Irish Sea, a facilty of greatly increased importance after the Danelaw treaty of 886, when it became the chief conduit for contact between the English kingdoms and such communities. Thus, although its location was somewhat dangerous – as the Ingimund episode demonstrated – it was also one endowed with many advantages in terms of commerce. The people here really were 'living on the edge.'

The sources mention or imply the stationing of naval forces at Chester at various times during the Anglo-Saxon and Anglo-Scandinavian eras. Aethelfrith possibly, and Edwin almost certainly, used it as a naval base in the seventh century; Edward and Aethelflaed did so in the early years of the tenth century during their campaigns against the Welsh, the Irish Vikings and the Danes; there is the reference to Edgar bringing a great fleet to the *burh* in 973; and further references to fleets operating from it in the eleventh century. It was of course Chester's possession of a natural harbour at the head of a sheltered estuary that influenced the Romans to choose Chester for the site of one of their great fortresses. This facility enabled supplies and raw materials to be brought in by sea (far easier and cheaper than doing so overland until the advent of powered transport in the modern era) and also enabled the equipping and mounting of amphibious military operations along the west coast of Britain. The military aspects of Chester's maritime role were, as we have seen, just as important in later centuries and this naval activity would have been one of the stimuli to its economic development through the spending power of the men who crewed the ships and the need to supply them with provisions.

The creation of the *burh* in 907 was a formal and tangible recognition of the city's renewed and increased military importance, but it also marked a step-change in Chester's economic development. The network of fortresses begun by Alfred was where royal power was concentrated, not simply military strength but also the regulation of trading activities to yield revenue and the control of coin production to guarantee the quality of the currency. Generally speaking, the output of a mint was a direct reflection of the prosperity of a town, so the fact that Chester became the most productive mint in the whole of England during the reign of Athelstan (924-39) is an indication of the amount of trade going on in Chester at that time and the wealth of its inhabitants. As described elsewhere in this chapter, the distribution of coins, pottery and decorated metalwork, along with the artistic styles of the latter, tell us much about the geographical extent of Chester's trading connections. Unsurprisingly this reinforces the impression gained from other evidence that the bulk of Chester's trade in this period was with Ireland, but also taking in the Isle of Man, Cumbria and the Western Isles. As far as can be discerned from the archaeological evidence the exports from Chester were essentially (comparatively) high-quality manufactured goods such as those just listed. In addition, salt from the mid-Cheshire -*wich* towns may have been exported via the port at Chester, perhaps packed in Chester-ware pots.[71] Apart from a few items of metalwork possibly manufactured in Ireland (though they could just as easily have been made by Norse-Irish working in Chester) imports into Chester are not represented in the archaeological record. The obvious conclusion is that these consisted largely of perishable goods and this is supported by the specific reference to marten-pelts in the port regulations recorded in Domesday. Quoted in full below, the regulation in question shows just how highly this particular commodity was prized, because the king's reeve had first option to buy them. Other commodities from Ireland presumably included other types of furs, livestock, grain and also slaves. As the Viking trading routes extended even further in the later tenth century, the imports into Chester could have included walrus ivory and other types of furs from the north along with rare luxuries such as wine and oil and silk and spices from the south.

The laws governing life in the *burh* as recorded in Domesday shed considerable light on mercantile trade and its management. Thus:

> If ships arrived at the City port or left port without the King's permission, the King and the Earl had 40 shillings from each man in the ship.

> If a ship arrived against the King's peace and despite his prohibition, the King and the Earl had both the ship itself and its crew, together with everything in it.

> But if it came with the King's peace and permission, those in it sold what they had without interference. But when it left the King and the Earl had 4 pence from each cargo; if the King's reeve instructed those who had marten-pelts not to sell to anyone until they were first shown to him and he had made his puchase, whoever did not observe this instruction was fined 40 shillings.

As to the location of the actual harbour facilities, in the early twelfth century these lay on the south side of the city just downstream from the Old Dee Bridge.

Alternatively, ships could have tied up in the 'portpool' area a few hundred metres downstream from the north-west extent of the *burh* defences, which became the main anchorage for the city by the late fourteenth century.[72]

AGRICULTURE AND THE RURAL POPULATION

The Domesday Survey lists the Norman owners of the manors or estates, their English owners in the time of King Edward (1066), along with their monetary value, the number of inhabitants (just the men, not their families) and details of their property, especially in terms of land or animals. Thus, in addition to the overall tax assessment and the heads of households on an estate, with indications of their status, the survey sets down such things as the area of plough-lands, meadow and woodland, along with special assets such as fisheries, mills and heys. A number of features distinguish Cheshire from neighbouring counties. First, there is the pre-eminence of the Mercian earl as landowner, for in addition to sharing the revenues from Chester itself and the salt towns of Middlewich, Nantwich and Northwich, he held nearly every important manor in the county. Second, the county was still relatively thinly populated. Even in the most densely settled area – the Dee valley – there were only about 15 people per square mile compared with 25–30 around other important marcher towns, such as Shrewsbury and Worcester. Large parts of the county were still covered by woodland, the Forest of Macclesfield in the east of the county and those of *Mara* (now Delamere) and *Mondrum* across large swathes of the central part of Cheshire.

The monks of St Werburgh's held a considerable number of middling-sized manors close to Chester as a result of successive gifts and endowments, as did St John's. Ownership of the remaining manors throughout the county was very varied. Most were of low value and held by a single individual. A few men acquired multiple holdings, some widely scattered, others more compact. Some individual owners are of interest. Leofnoth possessed the largest manors in north-west Wirral, centred on the Viking meeting-place at Thingwall, along with a scattering of others in the rest of Cheshire and a few across the Dee in modern Flintshire. His name appears on coins of the Chester mint and he may have been a relative of Earl Edwin. Both Tokig and Arni, holders of estates close to Chester, have names indicting Norse ancestry. Finally, fans of the 'Blackadder' series might be interested to learn that a Norman incomer called Baldric held property in Eddisbury.

The minor settlements existing in the vicinity of Chester at the time of the Domesday survey included Saughall, Blacon, Newton, Upton, Great Boughton, Christleton, Huntingdon, Waverton, Handbridge, Netherleigh, Marlston cum

Lache, Claverton and of course Eccleston. The last of these was, as we have seen, one of the earliest post-Roman settlements in Chester's immediate hinterland and the nearby site at Heronbridge has yielded archaeological evidence of agricultural activity (both flax and cereal growing) in the general area a century or more before the foundation of the *burh*. Agricultural activity in all of these communities is attested by the listing of ploughlands and meadowland, while the hamlet of Eaton, located beside the Dee just south of Eccleston, contained a valuable salmon fishery owned, as one might expect, by the earl.

Agricultural produce from the outlying farms would have been brought to market in Chester. Analysis of the animal bone from Anglo-Saxon contexts in Chester indicates a predominance of cattle, closely followed by pig, with sheep very much a poor third. Most of the cattle seem to have survived into maturity before being slaughtered, whereas the pigs were generally killed in their second year. Deer occur in the assemblage as both high- and low-meat bearing bones, suggesting they represent food waste as well as industrial debris. In Domesday, the description of manors with woodland also frequently mentions 'heys,' the enclosures used for driving deer. Rabbit and hare also formed part of the diet, as did chicken, duck, goose, woodcock and wood-pigeon, along with fish. Domesday also mentions 'eyries' from which young hawks could be taken to be trained for hunting, providing a pastime for the richer thegns as well as delicacies for the table.

THE POPULATION

As a bastion of Anglo-Saxon England interposed between Danes to the north and east, the Welsh to the west and the Norse across the Irish Sea, it might come as something of a surprise to discover that Chester's population – or at least its wealthier classes – was quite cosmopolitan from the earliest days of the *burh*. This is revealed by the names of the men who worked as moneyers in the city in the 920s and 930s. Thus of the 28 known, 12 were English, with names such as Aelfwin, Eadmund, or Wulfgar; six were Scandinavians, like Oslac and Thurstan, one was Irish (Maelsuthan), four possibly Frankish (including Boiga and Wiard); and two were Welsh (Paul and Martin). In other ways this is not so surprising as frontier towns tend to develop populations of mixed background, especially in circumstances such as those which obtained in North-West Mercia in the early tenth century, when there was an upsurge in commerce, especially between Chester and Viking Dublin.

The Scandinavian element in the population became even more significant over time as trade expanded through the next century and a half. This is reflected in the church dedications to St Bridget and St Olaf, the types and styles of decoration on a variety of everyday objects such as brooches and pins, and the naming of streets after individuals with Viking personal names. Further afield, there are the numerous Scandinavian (Norse rather than Danish) place-names, and even field-names, to be found across the Wirral: places such as Irby, Kirkby, Pensby and Whitby. Domesday reveals the use of Scandinavian land measures known as *ora* in Handbridge and this has been seen as supporting the notion that Scandinavians settling in Chester, being essentially a trading people, would have established themselves at the southern end of the city close to the river frontage. It is true that the two churches named after Scandinavian saints stood in the Lower Bridge Street area, as did the largest collection of cellared and semi-cellared buildings of essentially Viking form yet found in the city. But examples of this building type also occur inside the fortress, while pottery, metalwork and other artefacts of both Anglo-Saxon and Viking types are found both throughout the interior of the old Roman fortress and across all parts of the extramural area. There is no real evidence, therefore, for any segregation within the population. So while the proportion of English and Viking people probably varied from one part of the city to another, both sides apparently overcame the antipathy engendered by the Ingimund episode, put aside their differences, and evolved quite rapidly into an integrated Anglo-Scandinavian community.

GOVERNANCE

We know a great deal about the governance and prosperity of late Anglo-Scandinavian Chester owing to the recording in exceptional detail of the city's laws in Domesday Book. The *burh* was the administrative as well as the military centre for the district which supported its maintenance and, most importantly, from at least as early as 980 it was the seat of the court for the shire.[73] Justice was dispensed by this body which was presided over by 12 judges or doomsmen – the *iudices civitatis* – drawn from the men of king, earl and bishop. These men, who came from the 12 hundreds or divisions of Cheshire, were themselves liable to fines if they attempted to evade their responsibilities. Some have seen the 12 judges as evidence of Scandinavian influence on the city's institutions, equating them with the *lagemen* or *iudices* found in certain boroughs in the Danelaw, but this is doubted by others.[74]

The fines and penalties which could be imposed were severe but were considered necessary to impose order, to ensure that taxes were collected and to guarantee set standards of quality and measures in commercial transactions. Similarly, there were obligations to ensure the city's defences were properly maintained.

Thus:

The City of Chester paid tax on 50 hides in the time of King Edward. 3½ which are outside the City, that is 1½ beyond the bridge (Handbridge) and 2 hides in Newton and 'Redcliff' and in the Bishop's Borough, these paid tax with the City.

In the time of King Edward there were 431 houses in the City paying tax, and besides these the Bishop had 56 houses paying tax. This City then paid 10½ silver marks; two parts were the King's, the third the Earl's.

If the peace given by the King's hand, or by his writ of his commissioner, were broken by anyone, the King had 100 shillings thereby. But if the King's peace, given by the Earl on his orders, were broken, the Earl had the third penny of the 100 shillings which were given for it; and if the peace given by the King's reeve or the Earl's officer were broken, the fine was 40 shillings and the third penny was the Earl's.

If a free man, breaking the peace given by the King, killed a man in his house, his land and all his goods were the King's, and he became an outlaw himself. The Earl had the same (right), but only over his own man who paid this penalty. But no one could restore peace to any outlaw except through the King.

Whoever shed blood between Monday morning and Saturday noon was fined 10 shillings; but from Saturday noon to Monday morning the fine for bloodshed was 20 shillings. Similarly, whoever did so in the Twelve Days of Christmas, on Candlemas Day, on the first day of Easter, on the first day of Whitsun, on Ascension Day, on the day of the Assumption or of the Nativity of St Mary, or on All Saints' Day, paid 20 shillings.

Whoever killed a man on these holy days was fined £4; on other days, 40 shillings. Similarly, whoever committed breaking and entering or highway robbery on these Holidays and on a Sunday paid out a fine of £4; on other days 40 shillings.

Whoever committed collusion with a thief in the City gave up 10 shillings; but if reeve of the King or the Earl incurred this penalty, he paid 20 shillings.

Whoever committed robbery or theft or did violence to a woman in a house was fined 40 shillings for each of these [offences].

If a widow had intercourse with any one unlawfully, she was fined 20 shillings, but a girl 10 shillings for such an offence.

Whoever took possession of another's land in the City, and could not prove it to be his own, was fined 40 shillings; likewise whoever made a claim thereto, if he could not prove that it should be his.

Whoever wished to enter possession of his own or his kinsman's land paid 10 shillings. But if he could not or would not, the reeve received his land into the King's hand.

Whoever did not pay tribute at the due term was fined 10 shillings.

If a fire burnt the City, the man from whose house it came was fined 3 ora of pence and gave 2 shillings to his next door neighbour.

Two parts of all sums forfeit were the King's, the third part the Earl's.

Any man or woman who gave false measure in the City was fined 4 shillings when caught; similarly any one who made bad beer was either put in the dung-stool or paid 4 shillings to the reeves. The officer of the King or the Earl received this fine in the City, on whoever's land it was, whether the Bishop's or any other man's. Similarly with the toll; if anyone withheld it for more than three nights, he was fined 40 shillings.

In the time of King Edward there were 7 moneyers in the City, who paid £7 to the King and the Earl, additional to the revenue, when the coinage was changed.

There were then 12 judges in the City; they were from the King's, the Bishop's and the Earl's men. If any of them stayed away from the Hundred on a day when it sat without plain excuse, he was fined 10 shillings, [shared] between the King and the Earl.

For the repair of the city wall and the bridge, the reeve used to call out one man to come from each hide in the County. The lord of any man who did not come paid a fine of 40 shillings to the King and the Earl. The fine was additional to the revenue.

As well as the King and the Earl, the Bishop also received income from fines:

If a free man works on a Holiday, the Bishop has 8 shillings therefrom; from a male or female slave, however, who breaks a Holiday, the Bishop has 4 shillings.

If a merchant reaches the City, bringing a bale of goods, and opens it between Saturday noon and Monday, or on any other Holiday, without permission from the Bishop's officer, the Bishop has 4 shillings fine therefrom; if one of the Bishop's men finds any man loading within the City territory (on a Holiday) the Bishop has therefrom a fine of 4 shillings or 2 oxen.

There are other laws that deal specifically with the port and these are quoted in the next section.

It is clear from the foregoing that the city was controlled by three lords – king, earl and bishop – all of whom owned property there. The role of the earl was rather more prominent than in many other towns in other parts of England, a reflection of the unusual importance of the Mercian earls in the struggle against the Danes. In addition to the normal third share of a fixed tax he received a variety of other renders or tributes and was represented by an agent or reeve (*praepositus* or *minister*) who apparently had a status similar to that of the king's reeve. The Bishop of Lichfield was the third 'magnate' who, by 1066, held considerable property in the city including more than 50 houses, the manor of Redcliff, and the 'bishop's borough' including the complex of ecclesiastical buildings grouped around St John's church.

FROM CORONATION TO CONQUEST 975-1066

Only two years after his triumphant visit to Chester Edgar died and just three years later still, in 978, his son, Edward, was murdered. The crown then passed to the juvenile Ethelred II, whose reign was characterised by an inability to deal with a new series of Danish raids. The situation for those in Mercia was made worse by a series of vindictive acts against the Anglo-Scandinavian population by Ethelred, who suspected them of collaboration with the enemy. These of course merely served to alienate the inhabitants, paving the way for the eventual Danish victory. In 980, Cheshire – *Legeceaster scir* – was plundered by sea-raiders. The event is recorded in the Abingdon Chronicles, which described the raiders as 'a pirate host from the North' which suggests their origin was either Scandinavia or the Isles rather than Ireland.[1]

Chester probably escaped direct attack but the fact that the output of its mint declined indicates that it suffered economically along with the rest of the county. The situation was worsened by the levying of taxes and the confiscation of estates in order to raise the vast sums handed over to the Vikings as bribes or 'Danegeld' to stop them raiding the south and east. In 999 Ethelred's fleet used Chester as a base to support his attack on Strathclyde, although it also found time to attack the Isle of Man.[2] This fleet, again operating from Chester, later raided the Welsh in Mynyw. By 1013 Ethelred's rule had become so unpopular in the former Danelaw area of the north and east Midlands that they preferred to have Swein of Denmark as their ruler. Ethelred stayed in London and let his son Edmund lead his forces. In 1016, Edmund ravaged north-west Mercia, including Chester, because the population 'would not go out to fight the Danes'. Ethelred died the same year and Edmund and Cnut agreed to a partition of England, Cnut taking Mercia. Edmund died a mere 15 days after his father, leaving Cnut as king of all England.

Despite the displacement of the English ruling house, the ealdormanry of West Mercia was placed in the hands of the Mercian Leofwine and it passed from him to his son Leofric, Earl of Mercia 1030–57. The accession of Cnut ushered in a period of peace, social harmony and prosperity. His 'Scandinavian Empire' encompassed Denmark, Norway, Iceland and Scotland and the Isles as well as England, affording enormous scope for increased mercantile activity – a phenomenon in which Chester was to share. Cnut collected one enormous but final Danegeld which he used to pay off most of his army from Denmark. In 1018, at a great assembly at Oxford, he pledged to rule Danes and English alike, taking as his model the laws of King Edgar. As a further demonstration of his desire to make the two peoples into one nation he took Ethelred's widow, Aelfgifu, as his wife. However, he also maintained a mistress – another Aelfgifu, 'of Northampton', a member of one of the great Mercian families persecuted by Ethelred. Cnut had a son by each of these women, Harthacnut and Harald respectively.

With the accession of Cnut and the prosperous times that followed Chester's fortunes improved. As a safe anchorage on the west coast and the site of an important mint it was well placed to benefit from the increased mercantile activity in and beyond the Irish Sea. Its position was no doubt further enhanced by the prominence and influence of Leofwine and Leofric, successive earls of Mercia, and Chester was very probably the administrative and economic centre of the northern part of their territory. It is noticeable, for example, that the only churches in the north-west to appear in Florence of Worcester's list of religious houses enriched by Leofric are St John's and St Werburgh's. Another significant fact, highlighted by Higham, is the complete absence of royal estates in Cheshire at the time of the Domesday Survey, in contrast to the extensive and focal estates of the king in Shropshire and Staffordshire. Higham takes this to indicate that the delegation of royal authority in the north-west Midlands to an ealdorman (later earl) was supported by the transference of all royal lands associated with Chester but only a fraction of those belonging to Shrewsbury and Stafford.[3]

The peace fell apart after Cnut's death in 1036 and a struggle for power ensued between Harthacnut, aided by Earl Godwine of Wessex, versus Harald, supported by Earl Leofric. There was also trouble in the Marches where the Welsh had found a new and energetic leader in Gruffydd ap Llywelyn, who inflicted a major defeat on Leofric's army near Welshpool in 1039. As a consequence, Gruffydd took control of much of the land between the Clwyd and the Dee which had been in English hands for 300 years. Edward the Confessor came to the throne in 1040 but he was unable to stamp out the periodic outbreak of civil war, often involving one or more of the half-Danish sons of Earl Godwine. In 1055, Earl Tostig of Northumberland, one of the Godwine's offspring, fell out with Leofric's son Aelfgar, Ealdorman of East Anglia, and the latter was forced into exile. Taking up with a group of mercenaries from Dublin, Aelfgar joined Gruffydd in Wales and together they captured Hereford. Harold Godwineson retook the city for the King but Aelfgar was pardoned and shortly afterwards his Hiberno-Norse mercenaries sailed their fleet to Chester, where they were paid off. Two years later, around the time he succeeded his father as Earl of Mercia, he again called on the support of Gruffydd; possibly Edward and Harold Godwineson had tried to remove him. Aelfgar died five years later and the pair took the opportunity to move against Gruffydd. Earl Harold launched a surprise raid into North Wales and, taken unawares, Gruffydd just managed to escape from his palace at Rhuddlan. A more sustained campaign the following year led ultimately to Gruffydd being killed by his own followers. The land in north-east Wales which Gruffydd had taken returned to English control.

By 1065 Harold Godwineson was in *de facto* control of the kingdom and was merely awaiting the demise of the pious Edward to make his rule *de iure*. In the autumn of that year however there began a series of events that was to upset his plans. The Northumbrians rebelled against Harold's brother, Earl Tostig, and selected Morcar, Aelfgar's younger brother, as earl. They marched southwards and were joined by his brother, Earl Edwin, with an army composed of men from Mercia and from Wales. The King and Earl Harold acceded to their demands and Tostig was exiled. Thus, when King Edward died in January 1066, Harold's position was considerably weaker than it had been only a few months before. To strengthen ties with Mercia, the now King Harold took Edwin's sister Edith, widow of Gruffydd, as his wife. This new Queen of England, shortly to be widowed once more, was to hold this position for only a few months. As summer arrived Edwin and Morcar tried and failed to repel the landing by a Norwegian army under Tostig and Harold Hadrada in the Humber. It was soundly beaten by King Harold at the Battle of Stamford Bridge only a few days later, but of course Harold was to lose the next battle, and his life, when he fought William of Normandy at Hastings on 14 October. For a while, both Edwin and Morcar probably entertained thoughts of resisting the Norman advance but soon recognised the futility of so doing. They are likely to have attended William's coronation at Christmas, then were taken to Normandy by the King in the spring of 1067.

Opposition to William was most vigorous in Northumbria and also in parts of Mercia, most particularly in Cheshire and the Marches. Eadric 'the Wild', the owner of large estates in Shropshire, led a combined Mercian and Welsh attack on Hereford in 1067.[4] Orderic Vitalis, quoting William of Poitiers, who personally witnessed events in this period, refers to 'many lawless acts' perpetrated by the *Cestrenses* ('Chester-men') and Welsh, who at one point tried to evict William's supporters from Shrewsbury.[5] The Mercian aristocracy of north-west Mercia, with their headquarters at Chester, were the focus of opposition to William. It was also to Chester that Queen Edith supposedly retired after Hastings. The new king eventually moved to eliminate this resistance and so, late in the winter of 1069–70, William came north with an army which 'feared the wildness of the region, the severity of the winter, the scarcity of food, and the terrible ferocity of the enemy'.[6] Nonetheless, this army crushed the rebels and laid waste the surrounding countryside. The results of this are clear from the 'waste' condition of most of Cheshire, along with the neighbouring parts of Shropshire and Staffordshire, as described at the time of the Domesday survey in 1086. To consolidate his conquest he built castles at Chester and Stafford. When the rebellion was already well advanced Edwin and Morcar had managed to slip away from their 'hosts,' but they never managed to reach Chester. Morcar took up with Hereward the Wake and was taken when his revolt collapsed in 1071; Edwin ended up being slain by his own men when they recognised the cause was lost.[7]

ARCHAEOLOGY

The fluctuating fortunes of Chester's economy in this period are reflected by the output of coinage from the mint. There was a notable decline in the 980s followed by a modest revival in the following decade.[8] Chester's renewed role as a naval base in the opening years of the eleventh century no doubt helped to stimulate its economy, while the peace and prosperity brought about by Cnut's accession saw a marked increase in coin output during the period 1016–35, with at least 16 moneyers working in the city. The extent of the damage done to Chester and Cheshire's economy by the Viking incursion of 980 is unknown but a number of hoards buried around this time – that found near Pemberton's Parlour close to the northern spur wall and the recently discovered examples in rural locations near Heronbridge and Brereton – may have been associated with this episode. The evidence of Chester ware reveals a similar picture with a decline in the quantities reaching Dublin after c.1000 and there is a general consensus that after 1020 trade between England and Ireland was channelled via the Severn rather than the Dee.[9] This switch was probably encouraged to some extent by the successes of Gruffudd ap Llywelyn, King of Gwynedd 1039–63, which threatened the route along the North Wales coast, but was also part of a more general re-alignment of trading connections which was to see Bristol rise to pre-eminence among the ports of the western seaboard.[10] However, we should be careful not to paint too gloomy a picture of Chester's economy.

Any changes in the pattern of trade would have been gradual and the city still had many advantages. On the eve of the Norman invasion Chester was still a thriving provincial centre and an important military base, roles it was to retain for centuries to come. The set of regulations, taxes and fines set out in such exceptional detail in Domesday demonstrate the extent and importance of external trade while the information about the number of properties in the *burh* suggest a population somewhere in the region of 4,000.

Of the sites excavated so far only one has produced evidence for major change during this period. This is the Lower Bridge Street site where the planned development of houses erected soon after the *burh's* creation were demolished possibly some time before the end of the tenth century and the area subsequently given over to a leather industry.[11] It has to be admitted, however, that the dating evidence for this drastic change in land use is by no means conclusive and it is equally, if not more, likely that it happened as a consequence of the punishment meted out to the city for the prominent role it played in the rebellion against William of Normandy half a century later. The extent to which Chester suffered in the 'harrying of the North' is evident from the entry in Domesday which records that of the 487 houses standing in 1066, 205 had been lost. Similarly, the value of the annual payment to the state had been reduced by one third to £30 and the city was described as ' thoroughly devastated'.[12] The construction of the castle in the south-west corner of the *burh* must have been responsible for the destruction of some properties but there is reason to believe that the Norman impact upon the fabric of the city was both far more extensive and creative.

Because the frontages of the main streets of the city have been the scene of intense building activity since the Norman Conquest, usually including the provision of cellarage cut into solid rock, we have no way of telling what, if anything, was happening in these areas during the Anglo-Scandinavian era. The spread of buildings over much of the 'backland' areas coupled with the generally rather dispersed character of tenth and eleventh-century occupation suggests the street frontages were not heavily built up before 1066. It is also true that wherever pre-Conquest buildings have been examined the structural sequence did not continue into the post-Conquest period. There seems little doubt, therefore, that the closing years of the eleventh century saw a fundamental re-planning of the city within the defences. The basic street pattern was little affected; in point of fact it had to remain so because of the position of the gates. However, a system of long, narrow burgage plots stretching back from the street frontages was established with the dwellings and shops facing directly onto the street. This can be seen little changed on the first edition Ordnance Survey map of the city and, despite major changes in the backland areas, is still discernible throughout large parts of modern Chester.

Thus, there is little if anything visible today to testify to that vibrant period before the arrival of the Normans when the city was transformed from a decaying ruin into a thriving centre of commerce and trade. Yet it was events in this period that laid the foundations for Chester's future success. It is to be hoped that some of the proceeds of its present prosperity can be used to allow the story of this critical period in the city's development, and the associated artefacts, to be presented to the public.

BIBLIOGRAPHY

BEDE

Colgrave, B. & Mynors, R.A.B. (eds) 1969 *Bede's Ecclesiastical History of the English People.*
  Oxford University Press.

Plummer, C. 1896 *Venerabilis Baedae Opera Historica.* Oxford.

Sherley Price, L. 1955 *Bede's History of the English Church and People*, Penguin Classics.

THE ANGLO-SAXON CHRONICLE

Garmondsway, G.N. 1953 *The Anglo-Saxon Chronicle.* Everyman's Library.

Plummer, C. 1892 & 1900 *The Anglo-Saxon Chronicle: Two of the Chronicles Parallel*, based on an
  edition by J. Earle. 2 vols. Oxford.

CHARTERS

Birch, W. de Gray 1885-87 *Cartularium Saxonicum.* 3 vols. London.

Tait, J. (ed.) 1920 *The Chartulary of the Abbey of St Werburgh, Chester, Vol. 1.* Chetham Society 79.

Tait, J. (ed.) 1923 *The Chartulary of the Abbey of St Werburgh, Chester, Vol. 1.* Chetham Society 82.

FLORENCE OF WORCESTER

Thorpe, B. (ed.) 1848 *Florentii Wigorniensis, Chronicon ex Chronicis.* London: English Historical
  Society.

Simeon of Durham ed. T. Arnold 1882-5.

RANULPH HIGDEN

Lumby, J.R. (ed.) 1876 *Polychronicon Ranulphi Higden Monachi Cestrensis.* 2 vols. London:
  Longman.

Taylor, J. 1966 *The Universal Chronicle of Ranulf Higden.* Oxford.

ANNALES CESTRIENSES

Ainsworth, S. & Wilmott, T. 2005 *Chester Amphitheatre: From Gladiators to Gardens.* Chester:
  Chester City Council/English Heritage.

Alcock, L. 1967 'Excavations at Deganwy Castle, Caernarvonshire, 1961-6', *The Archaeol. Journ.*
  124, 190-201.

Alcock, L. 1971 *Arthur's Britain.* Harmondsworth.

Arnold, C.J. & Davies, J.L. 2000 *Roman and Early Medieval Wales.* Stroud: Sutton.

Barrow, J. 2001 'Chester's earliest regatta? Edgar's Dee-rowing revisited', *Early Medieval Europe* X, 81-93

Biddle, M. 1976 'Towns', in Wilson, D.R. (ed.), 99-150.

Binchy, D. 1962 'Patrick and his biographers, ancient and modern', *Studia Hibernica* II, 7-173.

Blackburn, M.A.S. (ed.) 1986 *Anglo-Saxon Monetary History.* Leicester University Press.

Blair, P.H. 1947 'The origins of Northumbria', *Archaeologia Aeliana* (4th ser.) 25, 28-37.

Boon, G.C. 1972 *ISCA: The Roman Legionary Fortress at Caerleon, Monmouthshire*. Cardiff. National Museum of Wales.

Buchanan, M., Jermy, K.E. & Petch, D.F. 1975, 'Watling Street in the grounds of Eaton Hall: excavations north of Garden Lodge, 1970-1', *Journ. Chester Arch. Soc.* (new ser.) 58, 1-14.

Bu'Lock, J.D. 1962 'The Battle of Chester', *Trans. Lancashire Cheshire Antiquarian Soc.* 72, 47-56.

Bu' Lock, J.D. 1972 *Pre-Conquest Cheshire, 383-1066*. Chester: Cheshire Community Council.

Cameron, K. 1968 'Eccles in English place-names', in Barley, M.W. & Hanson, R.P.C. (eds) *Christianity in Britain 300-700*. Leicester University Press.

Campbell, E. 1996 'The archaeological evidence for external contacts: imports, trade and economy in Celtic Britain AD 400-800', in Dark, K.R. (ed.), 83-96.

Carrington, P. 1975 'Some types of late Saxon pottery from Chester', *Cheshire Archaeological Bulletin* 3, 3-10.

Carrington, P. (ed.) 2002 *Deva Victrix: Roman Chester Re-assessed*. Chester: Chester Archaeological Society.

Chibnall, M. (ed.) 1969 *The Ecclesiastical History of Orderic Vitalis*. Vol. 2. Oxford.

Christie, R.C. (ed.) 1887 *Annales Cestrienses; or Chronicle of the abbey of St Werburgh at Chester*. Record Soc. Lancashire & Cheshire 14.

Colgrave, B. (ed.) 1985 *The Life of Bishop Wilfrid by Eddius Stephanus*. Cambridge University Press.

Dark, K.R. (ed.) 1996 *External Contacts and the Economy of Late Roman and Post-Roman Britain*. Woodbridge.

Dark, K. & Dark, P. 1977 *The Landscape of Roman Britain*. Stroud: Sutton.

Davies, E. 1933 'Excavations at Heronbridge. Appendix 1: Report on the human remains' *Journ. Chester Archaeol. Soc.* (new ser.) 33 Part 1, 46-8.

Davies, W. 1982 *Wales in the Early Middle Ages*. Leicester.

Dodgson, J. McN. 'Place-names and street-names at Chester', *Journ. Chester Arch. Soc.* (new ser.) 55, 29-62.

Dolley, R.H.M. 1955 'The Mint of Chester (Part 1): Edward the Elder to Eadgar', *Journ. Chester Archaeol. Soc.* (new ser.) 42, 1-20.

Dolley, R.H.M. 1960 'An unpublished Chester penny of Harthacnut from Caerwent', *Numismatic Chronicle* (ser. 6) 20, 191-3.

Dolley, R.H.M. & Pirie, E.J. 1964 'The repercussions on Chester's prosperity of the Viking descent on Cheshire in 980', *British Numismatic Journal* 33, 39-44.

Dornier, A. (ed.) 1977 *Mercian Studies*. Leicester University Press.

Edwards, N. (ed.) 1997 *Landscape and Settlement in Medieval Wales*. Oxford.

Edwards, N. & Lane, A. 1988 *Early Medieval Settlements in Wales AD 400-1100*. Bangor/Cardiff.

Edwards, N. & Lane, A. (eds) 1992 *The Early Church in Wales and the West*. Oxford.

Faulkner, N. 2000 *The Decline and Fall of Roman Britain*. Stroud: Tempus.

Fernie, E.C. 1986 'Anglo-Saxon lengths: the 'Northern' system, the perch and the foot', *The Archaeol. Journ.* 142, 246-54.

Fowler, P. 'Hillforts AD 400-700', in Jesson, M. & Hill, D. (eds) *The Iron Age and its Hillforts*. Southampton. 203-1.

Gardner, W. & Savory, H.N. 1964 *Dinorben*. Cardiff.

Gelling, M. 1988 *Signposts to the Past*. 2nd edn. Chichester: Phillimore.

Griffiths, D. 1996 'The maritime economy of the Chester region in the Anglo-Saxon period' in Carrington, P. (ed.) *'Where Deva Spreads her Wizard Stream': Trade and the Port of Chester. Papers from a Seminar held at Chester, November 1995*. Chester Archaeology Occasional Paper No. 3.

Groombridge, M.J. 1952 'The city-guilds of Chester', *Journ. Chester Archaeol. Soc.* (new ser.) 39, 93-108.

Hartley, B.R. 1954 'Heronbridge excavations: bronze-worker's hearth', *Journ. Chester Arch. Soc.* (new ser.) 41, 1-14.

Hartley, B.R. & Kaine, K.F. 1954 'Roman dock and buildings', *Journ. Chester Arch. Soc.* (new ser.), 41, 15-38.

Hawkins, E. (ed.) 1848 *The Holy Lyfe and History of Saynt Werburge of Henry Bradshaw.* Chetham Soc. 1st se. 15. Manchester.

Henderson, G.C. 1984 *Archaeology in Exeter 1983/4.* Exeter Museums Archaeological Field Unit.

Higham, N.J. 1993 *The Origins of Cheshire.* Manchester University Press.

Hill, D. 1969 'The Burghal Hidage: the establishment of a text', *Medieval Archaeology* 13, 84–92.

Hill, D. & Worthington, M. 2003 *Offa's Dyke: History and Guide.* Stroud: Tempus.

Hill, P. 2004 *The Age of Athelstan: Britain's Forgotten History.* Stroud: Tempus.

Hoffman, B. 2002 'Where have all the soldiers gone?' in Carrington, P. (ed.) 79–88.

Hogg, A.H.A. 1948 'The date of Cunedda', *Antiquary* 22, 201–5.

Jackson, K.H. 1969 *The Gododdin: The Oldest Scottish Poem.*

Jones, M. & Dimbleby, G. (eds) 1981 *The Environment of Man; The Iron Age to Anglo-Saxon Period.* Oxford: Brit Archaeol Rept 87.

Kirby, D.P. 1975 'Welsh bards and the border', in Dornier, A. (ed.), 31–42.

LeQuesne, C. 1999 *Excavations At Chester. The Roman and Later Defences Part I. Investigations 1978-90.* Chester Archaeology Excavation & Survey Reports No. 11. Chester: Chester City Council & Gifford & Partners.

Lloyd, J.E. 1939 *History of Wales.* 2 vols. London: Longman.

Macphail, R.I. 1981 'Soil and botanical studies of the "dark earth"', in Jones, M. & Dimbleby, G. (eds), 309–31.

Maddicott, J.R. 1989 'Trade, industry and the wealth of King Alfred'. *Past and Present* 123, 3–51.

Mason, D.J.P. 1985 *Excavations at Chester. 26-42 Lower Bridge Street 1974-6. The Dark Age and Saxon Periods.* Grosvenor Museum Archaeological Excavation and Survey Report No. 3. Chester: Chester City Council

Mason, D.J.P. 1987 'Chester: the canabae legionis', *Britannia* 18, 143–68.

Mason, D.J.P. 1994a 'The legionary bath-house', in Ward and Others, 18–20.

Mason, D.J.P. 1994b 'Hamilton Place 1971', in Ward and Others, 37–42.

Mason, D.J.P. 1998 'And the walls came tumbling down: excavations adjacent to the city walls in St. John Street, 1988/9', *Journ. Chester Arch. Soc.* (new ser.), 73, 11–20.

Mason, D.J.P. 2001 *Excavations at Chester. The Elliptical Building: An Image of the Roman World?* Chester Archaeology Excavation and Survey Report No. 12. Chester: Chester City Council.

Mason, D.J.P. 2001 *Roman Chester: City of the Eagles.* Stroud: Tempus.

Mason, D.J.P. 2005 *Excavations at Chester. The Roman Fortress Baths. Excavation and Recording 1732-1998.* Chester Archaeology Excavation & Survey Report No. 13. Chester: Chester City Council.

Matthews, S. 1999 'Archbishop Plegmund and the court of King Alfred', *Journ. Chester Arch. Soc.* (new ser.), 74 83–114.

Matthews, S. 2002 'St John's Church and the early history of Chester', *Journ. Chester Arch. Soc.* (new ser.) 76, 63–80.

Meyer, K. 1896 'Early relations between Gael and Brython', *Transactions of the Honourable Cymmrodorion Society*, 55–86.

Meyer, K. 1900 'Expulsion of the Dessi', *Y Cymmrodor* 14, 101–35.

Morris, R.H. 1894 *Chester in the Plantagenet and Tudor Reigns.* Privately published.

Morris, J. (ed) 1978 *Domesday Book 26. Cheshire.* Chichester: Phillimore.

Nash-Williams, V.E. 1950 *The Early Christian Monuments of Wales.* Cardiff.

Nelson, J.L. 1986 *Politics and Ritual in Early Medieval Europe.* London.

Nicholson, E.W. 1908 'The dynasty of Cunedag', *Y Cymmrodor* 10, 61–104.

Penney, S. & Shotter, D.C.A. 1996 'An inscribed Roman salt pan from Shavington, Cheshire', *Britannia* 27, 360–5.

Petch, J.A. 1933 'Excavations at Heronbridge', *Journ. Chester Archaeol. Soc.* (new ser.) 33 Part 1, 1–45.

Petch, D.F. 1998 'Cunedda and the foundation of Gwynedd', *Journ. Chester Arch. Soc.* (new ser.) 73, 21–30.

Pirie, E.J. 1964 *Grosvenor Museum, Chester, part 1: the Willoughby Gardner Collection of Coins with the Chester Mint-Signature.* London: Oxford University Press.

Richards, M. 1960 'Irish settlements in south-west Wales: a topographical approach', *Journ. Royal Soc. Antiquaries Ireland* 90, 133-62.

Savory, H.N. 1960 'Excavations at Dinas Emrys, Beddgelert, Caernarvonshire', *Archaeologia Cambrensis* 109, 13-77.

Schmidt, H. 1973 'The Trelleborg house reconsidered', *Medieval Archaeology* 17, 52-77.

Shoesmith, R. 1982 *Excavations on and close to the Defences*. London: Council British Archaeology Research Report 46: Hereford City Excavations 2.

Shotter, D.C.A. 2000 'Chester; the evidence of Roman coin loss', *Journ. Chester Arch. Soc.* (new ser.) 75, 33-50.

Skarre, K. 1976 *Coins and Coinage in Viking Age Norway*. Oslo: Universitets forlaget.

Stevens, C.E. 1961 *Sidonius Apollinaris*. Oxford.

Strickland, T.J. 1994 'The survival of Roman Chester: An overview', in Ward and Others. 5-17.

Swanton, M. (ed.) 2000 *The Anglo-Saxon Chronicles*. London: Phoenix.

Thomas, A.C. 1981 *Christianity in Roman Britain to AD 500*. London.

Thomas, A.C. 1994 *And Shall These Mute Stones Speak? Post-Roman Inscriptions in Western Britain*. Cardiff.

Thompson, F.H. 1962, 'Excavations in Nicholas Street, 1957', *Journ. Chester Archaeol. Soc.* (new ser.) 49, 1-4.

Thompson, F.H. 1969 'Excavations at Linenhall Street, 1961-2', *Journ. Chester Arch. Soc.* (new ser.) 56, 1-23.

Thompson, F.H. 1976 'The excavation of the Roman amphitheatre at Chester'. *Archaeologia* 105, 127-239.

Thornton, D.E. 2001 'Edgar and Eight Kings (AD 973): textus et dramatis personae', *Early Medieval Europe* X, 49-79.

Wainwright, F.T. 1942 'North-west Mercia 871-924', *Trans. Hist. Soc. Lancs. & Chesh.* 94, 3-56.

Wainwright, F.T. 1948 'Ingimund's Invasion', *English Historical Review* 63, 145-69.

Wainwright, F.T. 1975 *Scandinavian England*. Ed. Finberg, H.R. Chichester: Phillimore.

Wallace, P.F. 1986 'The English presence in Viking Dublin', in Blackburn (ed.), 201-21.

Walton, J. 1954 'The hogsback tombstones and the Anglo-Danish house', *Antiquity* 28, 68-77.

Ward, S.W. 1994a '1-11 Crook Street 1973/4', in Ward and Others, 21-7.

Ward, S.W. 1994b 'Goss Street, 1973', in Ward and Others, 28-36.

Ward, S.W. 1994c 'Hunter's Walk 1979 & 1980', in Ward and Others, 43-53.

Ward, S.W. 1994d 'Hunter Street School 1979 & 1981', in Ward and Others, 54-68.

Ward, S.W. 1994e 'Abbey Green 1975-8', in Ward and Others, 69-93.

Ward, S.W. 1994f 'Northgate Brewery 1972/3', in Ward and Others, 94-6.

Ward, S.W. and Others 1994 *Excavations at Chester. Saxon Occupation Within the Roman Fortress. Sites Excavated 1971-81*. Chester Archaeology Excavation & Survey Report No. 7. Chester: Chester City Council.

Webster, G. 1951 'Chester in the Dark Ages', *Journ. Chester Archaeol. Soc.* (new ser.) 38, 39-48.

Webster, G., Dolley, R.H. & Dunning, G.C. 1953 'A Saxon treasure-hoard found at Chester, 1950', *Antiquaries Journ.* 33, 22-32.

Webster, G. 1955 'A section through the legionary defences on the west side of the fortress', *Journ. Chester Archaeol. Soc.* (new ser.) 42, 45-7.

Williams, I. 1934 'Marwnad Cynddylan', *Bulletin Board Celtic Studies* 6, 134-41.

Wightman, E. 1985 Gallia Belgica. London: Batsford.

Williams, I. 1972 *The Beginnings of Welsh Poetry: Studies by Sir Ifor Williams* (ed. Bromwich, R.).

Wilson, D.R. (ed.) 1976 *The Archaeology of Anglo-Saxon England*. London: Methuen.

Wright, R.P. & Jackson, K.H. 1968 'A late inscription from Wroxeter', *Antiquaries Journ.* 48, 296-300.

NOTES

CHAPTER I

1 CIL 13 6780.
2 CIL 3 3228.
3 Mason 2005, 69-80.
4 Mason 2000, 143-6.
5 Mason 2001, 196-7.
6 ibid., 199.
7 Petch & Thompson 1959.
8 Mason 1995; 2001, 200-4; also LeQuesne 1999, 114-20.
9 See various articles in vols 1 & 2 new ser JCAS; Wright & Richmond 1955; RIB I Nos 445-573.
10 Mason 1987, 160-3.
11 Mason 2001, 190-1.
12 Thomas 1981.
13 H. Bradshaw, *Life of St Werburge of Chester*, Hawkins ed. 1848, 152.
14 See chapter 2.
15 Penney 1999; Penney & Shotter 1996; 2002.
16 Shotter 2000, 45.
17 Hoffman 2002.
18 Mason 1980.
19 Ainsworth & Wilmott 2005, 8.
20 Boon 1972, 97-8.
21 Thompson 1976, 152-4; Ainsworth & Wilmott 2005, 7.
22 Mason 2000, 146-9; 2005, 81-2.
23 Mason 2001, 213, Fig. 141.
24 Meyer 1900.
25 Meyer 1896; Richards 1960.
26 Nicholson 1908; Alcock 1971, 125-9; Blair 1947; Hogg 1948; Petch 1998.
27 *Codex Theodosianus* 7.4.28.

CHAPTER II

1 Campbell 1996; Arnold & Davies 2000, 172-6.
2 Nash Williams 1950.

3   Richards 1960; Davies 1982; Edwards & Lane 1992; Thomas 1994.
4   Winterbottom 1978.
5   Shertley-Price 1955.
6   Morris 1980.
7   Swanton 1996.
8   1969, 60.
9   Winterbottom 1978; Jackson 1982.
10 Dumville 1989.
11 See Kirby 1971.
12 Stevens 1961.
13 Binchy 1962.
14 Savory 1960; Gardner & Savory 1964; Alcock 1967; Fowler 1971; Alcock 1971, 209-23; Edwards & Lane 1988; Edwards 1997.
15 Northern Rescension of the ASC *sub anno* 547.
16 Wright & Jackson 1968.
17 Chadwick 1963, ch. 4.
18 Arnold & Davies 2000, 180-6.
19 1972, 18.
20 White & Barker 1998, 118-30.
21 White & Barker 1998, 126.
22 *Annales Cambriae*, Morris 1980, 85-91.
23 Mason 1994a; 2005, 83-6.
24 Zienkiewicz 1986 I, 262-8.
25 Richmond & Webster 1951.
26 Mason 1998; 2001, 213-15 with fig. 145; and forthcoming.
27 Strickland 1994; LeQuesne 1999, 99-107.
28 B.M. Harleian MSS 2071; Ralph Higden, *Holy Life and History of St Werburgh* (Chetham Soc os 15, 86); *Annales Cestrienses* 10 Christie ed. 1886, 11.
29 Wightman 1985, 292-3.
30 Cameron 1968; Gelling 1988, 96-9.

CHAPTER III

1   Nash-Williams 1950, No. 13.
2   The *Anglo-Saxon Chronicle* gives the date of the Battle of Chester as 604. But, as J.D. Bu'Lock pointed out (*Trans. Lancashire & Cheshire Antiquarian Soc.* 72, 47-56 especially 48 footnote 4) this was as the result of a naïve reading of Bede's statement that the battle took place 'shortly after' the synod (most probably held at Chester) at which the leaders of the British Church refused to accept the authority of Augustine. This date does not allow sufficient time for Edwin to grow to an age when he would have been capable of setting about constructing an alliance to regain his throne. The gap this created in Northumbrian history was filled in other sources by the childhood of Edwin. There is in fact another source which gives a date for the battle. This is the Welsh Easter Annals (*Annales Cambriae*) which says it took place in the year 170, which is equivalent to 613. Taking into account the dates for later events recorded in other sources the eminent historian John Morris (*Nennius. British History and the Welsh Annals,* Phillimore 1980, 44 & 46) considered that the initial entry in the Annals was for the year 447 rather than 444, which would thus place the Battle of Chester in 616.
3   1972, 40-1.
4   J A Petch 1933.
5   Davies 1933.
6   Hartley 1952; 1954, Hartley & Kaine 1954.

7   1951.
8   Bu'Lock 1972, 8.
9   Laing & Laing 1985.
10 Mason 2004.
11 Morris 1894, 490-5.
12 Holst 2004, 9.
13 Mason 2004, 80-4.
14 Buchanan, Jermy & Petch 1975, 9.

CHAPTER IV

1   1.22-23.
2   11.12, 28, 40.
3   Williams 1934.
4   Kirby 1975; Williams 1972, 122-54.
5   *ASC* 783.
6   Hill & Worthington 2003, 161-3.
7   According to a 'lost work' of Giraldus Cambrensis; Thacker 1982, 200.
8   *Annales Cestrienses* Gastrell MS.
9   1993, 102.
10 ibid.
11 1996, 53.
12 LeQuesne 1999.
13 Ward 1994e, 70-1, 83.
14 Ward 1994f, 94.
15 Ward 1994a, 30.
16 Macphail 1981; Dark & Dark 1997, 120-2; Faulkner 2000, 124.
17 Ward 1994d, 59.
18 Mason 2000.
19 Mason 1985, 2-6.
20 Mason 1985, 6-7.
21 Hodges 1981.
22 Mason 1980.
23 Ward 1990.
24 Mason 2001, 109-11; forthcoming.
25 Mason 2004.
26 SUERC 3764 and 3765.

CHAPTER V

1   For an excellent discussion of the factors which prompted raids see Walker 2000, 43-7.
2   Charter of Bishop Waerferth of Worcester.
3   Walker 2000, 77-79, 158-66 on relationship.
4   Matthews 1999.
5   Wainwright 1942, 12.
6   *Flores Historiarum* Coxe, H.O. ed. London 1841.
7   Dolley 1976, 356; Maddicott 1989, 41.
8   Mentioned as early as reign of Offa; Stenton 1971, 289.
9   Domesday Survey, i, f. 262b.
10 Wainwright 1942, 1948.

11 For latest discussion see Hill & Worthington 2004, 123-53.
12 Birch 1885-7, No. 1041; Tait 1920; Higham 1993, 182.
13 Thorpe ed 1848, 85. See also Thornton 2001, 49-79; Barrow 2001, 81-93; Nelson 1986, 302-3.
14 See Bu'Lock 1972, 56; Thacker 1982, 201; *contra* Walker 2000, 126.

CHAPTER VI

1 Dodgson 1968, 48; Thacker in VCH V ii, 222-3; churches Thacker, 133, 147.
2 Dodgson 1968, 49.
3 Hill 1969; 1981.
4 Fol. 272b.
5 Thompson 1969.
6 ed. 1994,
7 See most recently LeQuesne 1999.
8 See *Journal of the Chester Archaeological Society* vols 1 & 2.
9 Thompson 1969; Petch forthcoming; Webster 1955; Nicholas Street 1951; massive rubble and two cornice blocks.
10 1999, 120-1, 146-8.
11 Mason 1995; 2001; forthcoming.
12 One or more stretches of the west defences, heavy rubble including two fragments of moulded cornice from the wall were found in the fill of the fortress ditch at a depth of 8ft, Nicholas Street 1951 – Thompson 1962, 4.
13 Re-examination of the records of the 1966 Frodsham Street excavation show an identical sequence north of east gate.
14 As mentioned in chapter one there is a possibility that the western and perhaps even the southern suburbs of the fortress were enclosed by a defensive wall in the later Roman period.
15 Biddle 1976a, 130; 1976b, 27-8; Henderson 1984, 12-13.
16 Ward 1994f.
17 Ward 1994e.
18 Strickland 1994, 13.
19 Folio 263.
20 Mason 1985.
21 Huggins, Rodwell & Rodwell 1982, 21-5; but see also Fernie 1986.
22 Walton 1954; Schmidt 1973.
23 J.A. Rutter in Mason 1985, 64-5.
24 Mason 1994b.
25 Ward 1994a.
26 Ward 1994c.
27 Mason 2000.
28 Ward 1994c.
29 Ward 1994d, 58.
30 West 1969; Rahtz 1976; Blockley & Day 1981.
31 Ward 1994e.
32 Richmond & Webster 1951.
33 Ward 1988, 28.
34 Mason 1994a; 2005, 83-6.
35 D. Garner *pers. comm.*
36 D.W. Griffiths in Ward and others 1994, 103-4.
37 Griffiths 1994, 104.
38 G. Lloyd Morgan in Ward and others 1994, 98.
39 Sir David Wilson in Mason 1985, 61.

40 J. Graham-Campbell & G. Lloyd Morgan in Ward and others 1994, 66-7.
41 Graham-Campbell 1985, 448 pl. xcvii, c.
42 *The Past Uncovered,* June 2004.
43 G. Lloyd Morgan in Ward and others 1994, 98-9.
44 J. A. Rutter in Ward and others 1994, 102.
45 Q. Mould in Ward and others 1994, 107-8.
46 Rutter 1985.
47 Rutter 1988; 1994.
48 Wallace 1986; 1987.
49 Wallace 1986, 213; Shoesmith 1982, 45-55.
50 Rutter 1994, 86 and Fig. 9.13 No. 14.
51 Cooper 1892, 5.
52 Bu'Lock 1972, 77, 81-3; Bailey 1980, 177-82.
53 *Annales Cestriensis* Gastrell MS.
54 Fol. 263.
55 B.L. Harl. MS 2071; Higden, *Holy Life and History of St Werburg,* Chetham Soc. old ser. xv, 86;
   Annales Cestriensis 10.
56 Alldridge 1981, 11-16; Thacker 1987, 251-2, 268-71; 1988, 119-22.
57 Barlow, *Eng. Church 1066-1154,* 48.
58 D. Garner, *pers. comm.*
59 Webster, Dolley & Dunning 1953.
60 Graham-Campbell 1983, 63.
61 Dolley 1976, 356; Metcalf 1986, 143.
62 Graham-Campbell 1976, 48; Griffiths 1994, 125-7.
63 Wallace 1986, 213.
64 Pirie 1964; Dolley & Pirie 1964; Skarre 1976, 166; Rutter 1988, 31.
65 pers. comm. Dr A.J. Campbell.
66 Mason 1985, 23-6.
67 Groombridge 1952, 102-7.
68 Dodgson 1968, 43-5.
69 Ward 1994e.
70 Ward 1994e, 76-7, 83.
71 Oxley 1983.
72 Laughton 1996, 66-8.
73 See *VCH* Cheshire i 237; Higham 1993, 115.
74 Bu'Lock 1972, 70 contra Thacker VCH V.i 2003, 24.

CHAPTER VII

1 *ASC* C.
2 *ASC* E.
3 1993, 185-6.
4 *ASC* D.
5 Chibnall 1969.
6 Chibnall 1969, 234-6, 261.
7 *ASC* E.
8 Dolley & Pirie 1964.
9 Lloyd 1939, 2, 357-71; Dolley 1960, 191-3.
10 Wallace 1987, 231.
11 Mason 1985, 24-34.
12 DB.

INDEX